# Shakespeare: the 'lost years'

MANCHESTER
UNIVERSITY PRESS

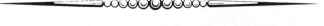

# Shakespeare: the 'lost years'

Second edition

## E. A. J. HONIGMANN

Manchester University Press

Manchester and New York

Distributed exclusively in the USA by St. Martin's Press

Copyright © E.A.J. Honigmann 1985, 1998

The right of E.A.J. Honigmann to be identified as the author of this work has been asserted by him in accordance with the Copyright, Designs and Patents Act 1988.

First edition published 1985 by Manchester University Press
Reprinted 1985

*This edition published 1998 by*
Manchester University Press
Oxford Road, Manchester M13 9NR, UK
*and* Room 400, 175 Fifth Avenue, New York, NY 10010, USA
http://www.man.ac.uk/mup

*Distributed exclusively in the USA by*
St. Martin's Press, Inc., 175 Fifth Avenue, New York,
NY 10010, USA

*Distributed exclusively in Canada by*
UBC Press, University of British Columbia, 6344 Memorial Road,
Vancouver, BC, Canada V6T 1Z2

*British Library Cataloguing-in-Publication Data*
A catalogue record for this book is available from the British Library

*Library of Congress Cataloging-in-Publication Data applied for*


ISBN 0 7190 5425 7 *paperback*

This edition first published 1998

05 04 03 02 01 00 99 98      10 9 8 7 6 5 4 3 2 1

Printed in Great Britain
by Biddles Ltd, Guildford and King's Lynn

# Contents

# List of plates

Plates I, III, IV, VII, VIII by courtesy of Sir Bernard de Hoghton, Bart., photos by Michael Scott; Plates V and IX (*b*) by courtesy of Lancashire Record Office, Preston; Plate IX (*a*) by courtesy of the Shakespeare Centre, Stratford; Plate IX (*c*) by courtesy of The British Library; Plates X–XII by courtesy of the Earl of Derby, photos by J.J. Bagley.

In the second edition Plate VIII has been replaced by reproductions of the de Hoghton coat of arms and crest (photos by Matthew Frost). The 'de Hoghton crest' reproduced in the first edition probably dates from the seventeenth century, too late for Thomas and Alexander Hoghton.

# Preface to the first edition

This book is really a detective-story, and the mystery it grapples with is one that experts have tried to solve for two hundred years. Where was young William Shakespeare in the so-called 'lost years' before 1592, and what was he doing? The correct answer, I believe, was first suggested by Oliver Baker in 1937 and then re-stated by E. K. Chambers in 1944[1] – namely, that the future dramatist served for a while in the household of a wealthy Roman Catholic land-owner in Lancashire. Chambers, our leading authority on Shakespeare in the present century, could not check some of the crucial documents in war-time but developed Baker's surprising theory (it almost certainly implied, among other things, that Shakespeare as a teenager was a practising Catholic), and, dying a few years later, left it to others to prove or disprove. After working on Lancashire archives for many years, in many places, I now publish an interim report on Shakespeare's 'Lancashire connection', a story that centres on the Hoghtons of Hoghton Tower but also throws light on other fascinating problems in the dramatist's later life.

Although I received some training in archive-work at the Shakespeare Institute (where I taught from 1951 to 1954) from our Senior Fellow, the late Professor C. J. Sisson, I have to confess that I felt then, and still feel, a mere dabbler as far as legal records are concerned. From Professor Sisson I learnt how to read almost illegible old manuscripts, and I found his delight in depositions (and demurrers etc.) infectious and irresistible. But, as he often observed, when you discover an interesting bill of complaint you rarely know the outcome or whether the case moved from one court to another: too many indexes for the Elizabethan period are incomplete, or totally chaotic and unhelpful. I mention this because it is perfectly possible that I have missed many opportunities, and that important records bearing on the 'Lancashire connection' still await discovery. I may also have made some mistakes in copying or correcting pedigrees from Baines and other authorities on Lancashire family history. In the sixteenth century husbands and wives often re-married, and the larger family might include twenty or more children, legitimate and illegitimate, with some Christian names repeating several times: it is only too easy, four hundred years later, to confuse two or more individuals with the same name. For these and other sins of omission and commission I apologise in advance.

Everyone who writes about Shakespeare borrows from earlier writers. I am particularly indebted to three studies, which have not had the acclaim they deserved: Oliver Baker's *In Shakespeare's Warwickshire and the Unknown Years* (1937), E. K. Chambers' 'William Shakeshafte' (in *Shakespearean Gleanings*, Oxford, 1944), and *The Annotator* by Alan Keen and Roger Lubbock (1954). I do not share the view, expressed in *The Annotator*, that William Shakespeare is responsible for the marginalia in the Newport copy of Halle's *Chronicle*, but found, when I turned belatedly to Keen's publications, that he had anticipated some of my ideas about Shakespeare and Lancashire. The present book differs from these predecessors in tracing, much more fully, the importance of Shakespeare's early patrons for his plays and poems; and I have burrowed more persistently in both public and private archives, in pursuit of the 'Lancashire connection', and have discovered law-suits, wills and other records, unknown to these earlier writers, that will affect future thinking about Shakespeare's social and intellectual background.

My debts to institutions and individuals have been incurred over several decades. I am grateful for the expert services of librarians and archivists in the British Library; the Public Record Office; the National Trust; the National Library of Wales; the Lancashire Record Office; the Cheshire Record Office; the Borthwick Institute, York; the Shakespeare Institute, Birmingham; the Shakespeare Centre, Stratford; the Bodleian Library; Christ Church Library, Oxford; Queens' College Library, Cambridge; Lambeth Palace Library; the College of Arms; the Goldsmiths Company; the Huntington Library; and, above all, Newcastle University Library. I am also most grateful to these libraries etc. for permission to quote from unpublished manuscripts in their keeping: the British Library, the Public Record Office, the National Library of Wales, the Lancashire Record Office, the Cheshire Record Office, Christ Church Library, the Goldsmiths Company and the Huntington Library. It is likewise a pleasure to record my debts to the following, who gave me advice and help of various kinds: Mr J. Blundell, Dr Susan Brock, Mr Barry Coward, Mrs S. Denyer, Professor D. W. Elliott, Mr P. Fleetwood Hesketh, Mr Levi Fox, the Dowager Lady Hesketh, Mr Roger Lubbock, Professor Brian Morris, Mr and Mrs Ashley Russell, Dr R. L. Smallwood, Mrs Iris Young. As always, I have to thank my wife for checking through my manuscript and proofs, and for correcting errors that I would have missed. I am also indebted to Miss Alison Foster, Miss Kathleen O'Rawe and Mrs Doris Palgrave, who helped me with the typing and took much trouble with a difficult manuscript; and to the University of Newcastle upon Tyne, for ten weeks of study leave, which gave me the time to complete this book. And I am deeply grateful to Professor John A. Cannon, Professor Harold Jenkins and Dr Alan Robinson, who read through my type-script and suggested many improvements.

I owe a special debt to D. L. Thomas and N. E. Evans of the Public Record Office, for permission to refer to their forthcoming paper on John Shakespeare, the dramatist's father; to G. C. G. Thomas of the National Library of Wales, for permission to see his schedule of the *Kinmel Deeds* and for expert advice on Lleweni and Salusbury records; and to J. J. Bagley, who allowed me to see a chapter from his forthcoming book on the Earls of Derby and helped me with 'Derby' problems. I am also indebted to the Earl of Derby, for permission to reproduce the portraits of the fifth and sixth Earls of Derby, and that of Lady Strange; and to Lord Hesketh, who allowed me to quote from the Hesketh archives and to visit the library at Easton Neston.

My greatest debt is to Sir Bernard de Hoghton, Bt., and to his mother (Mrs Richard Adams), for criticism and advice, for their generous hospitality, and for access to unpublished family archives. Also, for permission to include photographs of Hoghton Tower and Lea Hall, and other Hoghton material (Plates I, III–IV, VII–VIII).

Finally, several warnings to the reader. I have almost invariably modernised the spelling in quoting sixteenth- and seventeenth-century manuscripts and printed books, and also expanded contractions. Pointed brackets indicate that words or letters in the original are illegible; square brackets are used, in quotations from early texts, for editorial insertions. I have standardised names, as far as possible, even in quotations from early documents: the Stratford schoolmaster as John Cottom (his preferred spelling), though his father and brothers used the form 'Cottam'. The Hoghton family created special problems: in the sixteenth century the name appears as Houghton, Hoghton ›and de Hoghton. I usually standardise early references as Hoghton, even though de Hoghton is now the official spelling (resumed in the nineteenth century by Sir Henry de Hoghton, the ninth baronet, by royal licence).

Since so many of the men discussed in this book were Members of Parliament, I list below, in alphabetical order, those with biographies in P. W. Hasler's *The House of Commons 1558–1603* (3 vols, H.M.S.O., 1981). Though some of Hasler's contributors are not as reliable as one might have wished (see below, p.15: Sir Richard Hoghton), it is useful to alert the reader to the fact that we have detailed (and, normally, up-to-date) accounts of some of the principals and of some minor figures in our story. These include Sir Robert Cecil, John Fleetwood, Sir Gilbert Gerard, Sir Thomas Gerard, Sir Thomas Heneage, Edward Herbert (Lord Herbert of Cherbury), Robert Hesketh of Rufford, Thomas Hesketh (Alexander Hoghton's brother-in-law), Sir Richard Hoghton, Thomas Langton (baron of Newton), Sir Peter Leigh, Sir Richard Lewkenor, Sir Richard Molyneux, Sir Walter Raleigh, Sir John Salusbury, Sir Robert Salusbury, Simon Thelwall, Sir Edmund Trafford, Sir John Trevor, Sir Richard Trevor, William Waad, Sir Edward Warren.

# Preface to the second edition

How did the world react to *Shakespeare: the 'lost years'* in 1985 and thereafter? For a few weeks the 'media interest' went far beyond my expectations: the author was interviewed on the radio, on television and in newspapers. An educational programme made by Yorkshire Television for Channel 4, entitled 'A Tudor Interlude' (written by Freda Kelsall, produced and directed by Ian Fell), was transmitted three times in Britain, in 1993, 1994 and 1995, and also issued on video by Yorkshire–Tyne Tees Enterprises Ltd., with the following publicity material:

> Master William Shakeshafte (guess who?) is responsible for the Catholic education of young Dick Hoghton in a household torn by opposition to the state religion. This exciting three-part drama involves the hunt for travelling priest Edmund Campion, the mounting of a masque about Drake, and a border skirmish which threatens the family succession. Supporting documentaries search for evidence behind the dramas, which were inspired by E. A. J. Honigmann's *Shakespeare: the 'lost years'* ...

The Teachers' Guide associated with this programme sold 10,000 copies – more than *Lost Years* itself, such is the power of television.

Quite naturally the academic world reacted with more caution. The foremost Shakespeare biographer of the later twentieth century, Samuel Schoenbaum, nevertheless accepted that the 'Lancashire connection' could no longer be ignored.

> The present book makes it no longer possible for the responsible biographer to avoid a detour, with Honigmann for his *Guide Michelin*, into Lancashire, a long way from Stratford ... Honigmann's book opens doors. Who knows, after over four centuries, what unsuspected treasures remain to be discovered? (*Times Literary Supplement*, 19 April 1985)

This, of course, has been my position from the beginning. The book is an 'interim report' (p. vii); 'I do not claim that all the suggestions in the book are equally probable' (p. 127) – though I did think, and still think, that they all deserve further investigation; 'more work needs to be done before we shall discover all we want to know about the school-master in the country' (p. 132).

Two years later, in the 1987 edition of his *William Shakespeare: A Compact Documentary Life*, Schoenbaum wrote, more negatively, that

> if Shakespeare was at seventeen in Hoghton's service, he would have had to be back in Stratford to woo, impregnate, and marry Anne Hathaway before his nineteenth birthday, not – on the face of it – the most plausible of scenarios.[1]

Compare *Lost Years*, p. 39. Yet in a 'Postscript' to the same book Schoenbaum added, less negatively,

> With respect to the will of Alexander Hoghton ... Professor David George, who

has been collecting and editing the Lancashire materials for the *Records of Early English Drama* series, notes that Hoghton's musical instruments in fact no doubt went to Sir Thomas Hesketh ... as may be seen from the inventory of the property of his son Robert drawn up in 1620. Most likely Sir Thomas accepted both instruments and players – Fulke Gyllome surfaces as a Hesketh servant in 1591.[2]

Before I mention some of the new work that appeared after 1985 I must refer to one book published earlier, Peter Milward's *Shakespeare's Religious Background* (1973). As indicated below (pp. 3–6), E. K. Chambers's paper on 'William Shakeshafte' and T. W. Baldwin's discussion of John Cottom both appeared in 1944, each apparently written in ignorance of the other. Milward saw that if Shakespeare was indeed in his younger years a school-master in the country, Cottom (or Cottam) and Shakeshafte both point in the same direction:

> of the five schoolmasters at Stratford three were from Lancashire, Walter Roche, John Cottam and Alexander Aspinall. Of the three John Cottam, in particular, had been a neighbour of Alexander Houghton at Lea Hall; and it was during his brief tenure of office that Derby's players were twice entertained at Stratford for the festivities after Christmas. It may therefore have been in company with these players that the young Shakespeare was first sent north by his father, bearing a letter of introduction from the schoolmaster to Alexander Houghton. (pp. 41–2)

This is not quite the same as my guess that young William Shakespeare was recommended to Alexander Hoghton as an assistant teacher, and was drawn into 'playing' thereafter, yet Milward seems to have been the first to recognise how the 'Lancashire' clues in Shakespeare's biography support one another. Milward did not pursue these clues in the Lancashire archives, and I differ from his view, more positively expounded in his later book, *The Catholicism of Shakespeare's Plays* (1997),[3] that the plays contain a 'hidden, allegorical-topical meaning' sympathetic to the Jesuits and Rome (Mr Milward is himself a Jesuit). On the contrary, as I explain (pp. 119 ff.), the author of plays like Parts 1 and 2 of *Henry VI* and *King John* could hardly have been more hostile to Rome, although his surprising slip in *Hamlet*, where he wrote as if accepting the Catholic doctrine of Purgatory, suggests that he may have been a lapsed Catholic, one who had not wholly disembarrassed himself of Catholic eschatology. That said, Milward saw – more clearly than any predecessor named elsewhere in this book (pp. vii, 3, 40 ff.) – that Shakespeare's biographers must make a detour into Lancashire, and I regret that I did not acknowledge this in the first edition.

After 1985 I received letters from many readers of *Lost Years*, most of them complete strangers, with suggestions both more and less helpful, some of which may yet yield interesting results. Published 'follow-up' work and independent research have also been mixed, both positive and negative. It was encouraging that the Oxford editors included the Shakespeare epitaphs in the *Complete Works* (Oxford, 1986, p. 887), and that Peter Thomson decided that Ferdinando, Lord Strange, 'might well have been Shakespeare's most influential patron' (*Shakespeare's Professional Career*, Cambridge, 1992, p. 40). In addition, Gary Taylor has suggested that a seventeenth century manuscript miscellany, which contained a version of Shakespeare's second sonnet, may have been compiled by Mary Hoghton, the sister of Sir Richard Hoghton of Hoghton Tower.

'This connection is particularly intriguing, because the Hoghton family in the 1580s has been conjecturally linked with Shakespeare.'[4]

A chapter in David Honneyman's *Closer to Shakespeare*,[5] entitled 'Shakespeare in Lancashire – New Straws in the Wind', begins by stating that 'E. A. J. Honigmann went into the whole question and made a fairly good case for it', then, I was sad to find, disagrees with most of my suggestions. 'I assume that Shakespeare perhaps went to Lancashire not as a schoolmaster but as a page, household servant, or player (the last being the most likely) and that he went when he was quite young, say about 14'; 'if he was recommended by a schoolmaster, it was not by Cottom but by Walter Roche'. Roche, Cottom's predecessor as Stratford's schoolmaster, was certainly a Lancastrian, yet Lancashire is a large county and I know of no evidence that connects Roche and the Hoghton family. Here it may be appropriate to mention what several correspondents have pointed out to me – that, despite the distance between the Stratford area and Lancashire, a number of families owned land etc. in both and might have persuaded Alexander Hoghton to employ young William Shakespeare.

Most of the chapters in *Lost Years* have won some support, with one exception. The chapter on *The Phoenix and the Turtle* seems to have struck reviewers as far-fetched. In self-defence I would say that all interpretations of this poem have impressed others as far-fetched. It is a difficult, elusive poem – if its interpretation were a straightforward matter argument would have ceased long ago. Reviewers were uneasy about my early date for the poem, because 'Shakespeare could not have written like this in 1586.'[6] How do they know? As he wrote no other poems in the same strange vein their verdict (which was foreseeable: *Lost Years* 100–1) leaves me unmoved. I believe that Shakespeare, like other great artists, is unlikely to have been a late developer; for a special occasion the young Shakespeare might make a special effort, and *The Phoenix and the Turtle* was surely written by a poet determined to dazzle. Too good for Shakespeare at the age of twenty-two? He was already married, the father of three children, he had to make his way in the world, we know that he courted the favour of influential patrons later in his career – why not in 1586? This date explains so many mysterious allusions in the poem, puzzles that are simply ignored by other explicators, that I continue to think that 'The Phoenix and the Turtle' could have been the work of a very brilliant young poet, one capable of breaking new ground (when was this *not* true of Shakespeare?).

It is only fair to warn readers that there are traditionalists who disagree with other parts of *Lost Years*. My 'Conclusion', where I suggest (pp. 128–9) how the 'Lancashire connection' ties in with the chronology of Shakespeare's later career, displeases those who believe that his earliest extant plays date from 1590 (the 'late start' theory), since I date his first play *c.* 1586 (the 'early start'). I must therefore stress that the 'Lancashire connection' by no means necessitates either an early or a late start: in either case we have a gap of some years between Shakespeare's supposed sojourn in Lancashire and his earliest plays. But as my Shakespeare chronology has caused some misunderstanding, partly because, as I took care to point out, 'I have not assigned a date to every play' (*Lost Years*, p. 128), I subjoin my dates for all the extant plays and poems up to 1600: 1586 *Titus Andronicus*; 1587 *The Two Gentlemen of Verona*; 1588 *1 Henry VI, The Taming of the Shrew*; 1589 *The Comedy of Errors, 2 Henry VI*; 1590 *3 Henry VI, Richard III*; 1591 *King John, Romeo and Juliet*; 1592 (plague) *Love's Labour's Lost*; 1593 (plague)

*Venus and Adonis*; 1594 (plague) *The Rape of Lucrece*; 1595 *A Midsummer Night's Dream, Richard II*; 1596 *1 Henry IV, The Merchant of Venice*; 1597 *The Merry Wives of Windsor, 2 Henry IV*; [?1597–1600 *The Sonnets*]; 1598 *Much Ado About Nothing, Henry V*; 1599 *Julius Caesar, As You Like It*; 1600 *Hamlet*.[7] A supporter of the 'late start' chronology has objected that, according to my 'early start', Shakespeare 'wrote eleven plays in the five years between 1586 and 1591' and 'only five plays in the seven years between 1591 and 1598',[8] and called this a surprising disparity. I do not follow his arithmetic and would maintain, on the contrary, that – leaving aside the plague years, and even the likelihood that some of my dates may err by a year or so – Shakespeare's output seems remarkably steady. The same critic commented on Greene's 'upstart crow' (see *Lost Years*, pp. 69–71):

> That Greene would have used this contemptuous language, with its clear implication that its object is a Johnny-come-lately trying to imitate his betters, in reference to an established playwright with eleven plays to his credit ... defies belief. (*ibid.*)

The 'Johnny-come-lately' is a figment of the imagination. Greene, addressing 'those Gentlemen his Quondam acquaintance, that spend their wits in making plaies' (*Groat's Worth of Wit*, 1592), refers to Shakespeare as an upstart crow because Shakespeare was an actor and not a gentleman (unlike Greene and his quondam acquaintances, who seem all to have been university graduates, therefore 'Gentlemen'). The crow is a social upstart, not a newcomer. Greene does, however, give us some help in dating Shakespeare's arrival in London when the 'upstart crow' passage modulates into the fable of the grass-hopper and the ant (= Greene and Shakespeare).[9] The grass-hopper 'went for succour to the Ant his olde acquaintance': if Shakespeare was a newcomer, is it likely that Greene would have described him as an old acquaintance?

The very thorough sifting of local archives in the Lancashire volume of *Records of Early English Drama* (ed. David George, 1991) has not added to the information already available in *Lost Years*. The same is true of a slighter volume, a labour of love by a retired Lancashire lawyer, Graeme Bryson's *Shakespeare in Lancashire* (1997).[10]

Finally I must mention *John Weever: A biography of a literary associate of Shakespeare and Jonson* (Manchester, 1987), which includes the 'new edition of Weever's *Epigrammes*' announced as forthcoming on p. 52, below. In this later study I traced the many contacts of Weever's family with Sir Richard Hoghton's, the most extraordinary being Weever's 'affection to the dear memory' of Thomas Langton, who had been responsible for the death of Thomas Hoghton II, Sir Richard's father. We learn of this relationship from two unpublished manuscript notes that have survived in Weever's papers (*John Weever*, pp. 6–11).

A second matter of interest to students of Shakespeare's 'Lancashire connection' is Weever's penchant for 'in' jokes about his Cambridge friends and enemies (*John Weever*, pp. 12–16). This lends some support to the suggestion (*Lost Years*, p. 54) that Weever's lines on Shakespeare are another 'in' joke, being written in the form of a Shakespearian sonnet.

Weever's smallness, to which he himself drew attention twice in *Ancient Funeral Monuments* (*John Weever*, pp. 42–3), helps to identify him as a not insignificant participant in the War of the Theatres. Dekker later depicted him in *Satiromastix* (1601) as a hanger-on of Jonson called Asinius Bubo, whose smallness, begging habits and partiality for tobacco are repeatedly jeered at.

> *Asin.* Morrow, Captain Tucca, will you whiff this morning?
> *Tucca.* Art thou there, goat's pizzle? no, godamercy, Cain, I am for no whiffs, I; come hither, *sheep-skin-weaver*, s'foot thou look'st as though thou'dst begged out of a jail … draw near: this way, march, follow your commander, you scoundrel.

The same jeers are already found in Jonson's *Every Man in his Humour.*

> I cannot tell, but (vnles a man had iuggled begging all his life time, and beene a *weaver of phrases* from his infancie, for the apparelling of it) I thinke the world cannot produce his Riuall.[11]

According to Herford and Simpson, *Every Man in his Humour* was first produced 'about the middle of September, 1598'.[12] If I am correct in thinking that Weever left Cambridge for London in April, 1598 (*John Weever*, p. 2, 21) his dwarfish stature and other unusual characteristics seem to have drawn attention to him very quickly. That Jonson slapped him down in September, 1598, therefore bears on the dating of *Epigrammes*, and of Weever's verses on Shakespeare. As Weever himself explained (*Lost Years*, pp. 54–5), his *Epigrammes* were penned a year before they were printed: his flattering verses addressed jointly to Jonson and Marston, which are likely to have antedated the War of the Theatres, once again confirm that most of the *Epigrammes* will have been written by September, 1598, and also that in his lines on Shakespeare he may well have been the very first 'insider' to identify some of Shakespeare's plays by name, perhaps preceding even Francis Meres's *Palladis Tamia* (S.R. 7 September, 1598). Consequently one asks, 'Did Weever have access to the *Sonnets* in 1598? How did he get to know Shakespeare so quickly?'

The poem, 'A Memento for Mortality', with its echoes of *Hamlet* (*Lost Years*, pp. 57–8), first appeared in print in William Basse's *A Help to Discourse*, a miscellany issued in 1619, and Weever's authorship must therefore be regarded as uncertain (*John Weever*, pp. 65–6).

See also Richard Wilson, 'Shakespeare and the Jesuits: New connections supporting the theory of the lost Catholic years in Lancashire' (*Times Literary Supplement*, December 19, 1997, pp. 11–13).

# Notes

1 Schoenbaum, *op. cit.*, p. 115.
2 Schoenbaum, *op. cit.*, p. 324. Yet Schoenbaum's afterthought merely repeated *Lost Years*, pp. 31–3.
3 Renaissance Monographs, no. 23, published by the Renaissance Institute of Sophia University, Tokyo, 1997.
4 'Some Manuscripts of Shakespeare's Sonnets' (*Bulletin of the John Rylands Library*, 1985–6, pp. 210–46).
5 Merlin Books, Braunton, Devon (n.d.).
6 But compare Peter Thomson: *The Phoenix and the Turtle* 'may date from the 1580s …

There seems little reason to doubt that Shakespeare wrote with facility from an early age' (*op. cit.*, p. 22).

7 See my *Shakespeare's Impact on his Contemporaries* (1982), pp. 53–90, and, for the *Henry IV* plays and *Merry Wives*, 'Sir John Oldcastle: Shakespeare's martyr' (in '*Fanned and Winnowed Opinions*', ed. John W. Mahon and Thomas A. Pendleton, 1987, pp. 118–32).

8 Sidney Thomas, 'On the Dating of Shakespeare's Early Plays' (*Shakespeare Quarterly*, 1988, vol. 39, pp. 187–94).

9 For the grass-hopper and the ant see my *Shakespeare's Impact*, pp. 1–6.

10 Sunwards Publishing, Hightown, Liverpool. I am grateful to Sir Bernard de Hoghton for drawing my attention to this pamphlet, and for lending me his copy.

11 This is from the Quarto text: *Ben Jonson*, ed. C. H. Herford and Percy and Evelyn Simpson (11 vols., Oxford, 1925–52), III, 239. My italics.

12 *Ben Jonson*, I, 18.

# List of abbreviations

The following abbreviations have been used for periodicals, the publications of learned societies, works of reference, libraries, etc.

APC—*Acts of the Privy Council of England*, ed. J. R. Dasent etc., 1890– . (All references are to the reign of Queen Elizabeth I, unless otherwise stated.)

BL—The British Library (formerly British Museum).

CRS—*Catholic Record Society.*

CS—*Chetham Society.*

DD (etc.)—Documents in the Lancashire Record Office; thus DDHo refers to the Hoghton archives; DDHe to the Hesketh archives, etc.

DL (etc.)—Duchy of Lancaster records in the Public Record Office.

DNB—*Dictionary of National Biography.*

EHR—*English Historical Review.*

HMC—Historical Manuscripts Commission.

HSLC—*Transactions of the Historic Society of Lancashire and Cheshire.*

LRO—Lancashire Record Office.

MLR—*Modern Language Review.*

PCC—Prerogative Court of Canterbury (all PCC wills are in the Public Record Office).

PRO—Public Record Office.

Req—Court of Requests.

RES—*Review of English Studies.*

RSLC—*Record Society of Lancashire and Cheshire.*

Sh. Survey—*Shakespeare Survey.*

SPD—*State Papers Domestic.* (When two numbers follow *SPD*, these indicate the volume and document numbers. All references are to the reign of Queen Elizabeth I, unless otherwise stated.)

S. R.—The Stationers' Registers (cited from *A Transcript of the Registers of the Company of Stationers of London; A. D. 1554–1640.* Edited by Edward Arber. Five vols. London, privately printed, 1875 etc.).

Works frequently referred to are sometimes quoted by short title only: the full titles will be found in the list below. The place of publication is London where not otherwise stated.

Baker, *In Shakespeare's Warwickshire*—*In Shakespeare's Warwickshire and the Unknown Years.* By Oliver Baker. 1937.

Baldwin, *Small Latine*—*William Shakspere's Small Latine & Lesse Greeke.* By T. W. Baldwin. 2 vols. Urbana,University of Illinois Press. 1944.

Brown, *Salusbury and Chester*—*Poems by Sir John Salusbury and Robert Chester.* With an introduction by Carleton Brown. (Early English Text Society. Extra Series, no. CXIII (for 1913.)) 1914.

Chambers, *Gleanings*—*Shakespearean Gleanings.* By E. K. Chambers. Oxford. 1944.

Chambers, *Shakespeare*—*William Shakespeare: A Study of Facts and Problems.* By E. K. Chambers. 2 vols. Oxford. 1930.

Chambers, *Stage*—*The Elizabethan Stage.* By E. K. Chambers. 4 vols. Oxford. 1923.

# List of abbreviations

Coward, *The Stanleys—The Stanleys Lords Stanley and Earls of Derby 1385–1672*. By Barry Coward. (*CS*, 3rd Series, XXX.) Manchester, 1983.

Fishwick, *Preston—The History of the Parish of Preston*. By Henry Fishwick. 1900.

Gillow, *English Catholics—A Literary and Biographical History, or Bibliographical Dictionary of the English Catholics*. By Joseph Gillow. 5 vols. 1885 etc.; Burt Franklin reprints, New York.

Gillow, *Map—Lord Burghley's Map of Lancashire in 1590*. By Joseph Gillow. London. Privately printed, 1907. Also in *CRS*, 1907, IV, 162 ff.

Hasler — *The House of Commons 1558–1603*. By P.W. Hasler. 3 vols. H.M.S.O. (the History of Parliament Trust). 1981.

*Henslowe's Diary—Henslowe's Diary*. Edited by R.A. Foakes and R.T. Rickert. Cambridge. 1961.

Hotson, *Shakespeare's Sonnets Dated — Shakespeare's Sonnets Dated and other Essays*. By Leslie Hotson. 1949.

Keen, *The Annotator—The Annotator: The Pursuit of an Elizabethan Reader of Halle's Chronicle Involving some Surmises about the Early Life of William Shakespeare*. By Alan Keen & Roger Lubbock. 1954.

Leatherbarrow, *Elizabethan Recusants — The Lancashire Elizabethan Recusants*. By J. Stanley Leatherbarrow. (*CS*, New Series, CX.) 1947, reprinted 1968.

Lefranc, *Sous le Masque — Sous le Masque de 'William Shakespeare': William Stanley VIe Comte de Derby*. By Abel Lefranc. 2 vols. Paris. 1918.

Lumby, *Calendar—A Calendar of the Deeds and Papers in the Possession of Sir James de Hoghton, Bart., of Hoghton Tower, Lancashire*. By J.H. Lumby. (*RSLC*.) 1936.

Miller, *Hoghton Tower—Hoghton Tower: The History of the Manor, the Hereditary Lords and the ancient Manor-house of Hoghton in Lancashire*. By Geo. C. Miller. Preston. 1948.

*Nashe—The Works of Thomas Nashe*. Edited by R.B. McKerrow (re-edited by F.P. Wilson). 5 vols. Oxford. 1958.

Schoenbaum, *Documentary Life—William Shakespeare: A Documentary Life*. By S. Schoenbaum. Oxford. 1975.

Schoenbaum, *Lives—Shakespeare's Lives*. By S. Schoenbaum. Oxford. 1970.

*Sh. Encyclopaedia—A Shakespeare Encyclopaedia*. Edited by Oscar James Campbell and E.G. Quinn. 1966.

Smith, *Calendar of Salusbury Correspondence—Calendar of Salusbury Correspondence 1553—circa 1700*. Principally from the Lleweni, Rug and Bagot Collections in the National Library of Wales. Edited by W.J. Smith. (Board of Celtic Studies, University of Wales. History and Law Series, no. XIV.) 1954.

*Stanley Papers, The, Part II—The Stanley Papers. Part II. The Derby Household Books; comprising an Account of the Household Regulations and Expenses of Edward and Henry, Third and Fourth Earls of Derby (by W. Farington)*. Edited by F.R. Raines. (*CS*, XXXI.) 1853.

Tait, *Quarter Sessions—Lancashire Quarter Sessions Records. Vol. I. Quarter Sessions Rolls 1590–1606*. Edited by James Tait. (*CS*, New Series, LXXVII.) 1917.

*Visitation, 1613—The Visitation of the County Palatine of Lancaster. Made in the Year 1613, by Richard St. George, Esq., Norroy King of Arms*. Edited by F.R. Raines. (*CS*, LXXXII.) 1871.

# I

## Introduction

Where was William Shakespeare in the 'lost years' before 1592, and how did he make a living? Apart from the records of his baptism (26 April 1564) and licence to marry (27 November 1582), and of the christening of his children, Susanna (26 May 1583) and the twins Hamnet and Judith (2 February 1585), the rest is silence. Then Robert Greene attacked Shakespeare in September 1592, as an upstart crow in the theatrical world, one who 'supposes he is as well able to bombast out a blank verse' as the best contemporary dramatists, and 'being an absolute Johannes factotum, is in his own conceit the only Shake-scene in a country.' Aged 28, Shakespeare is not a complete newcomer on the literary scene, for Robert Greene, one of the most popular writers of the previous decade, regards him as a serious threat; but how long had he been writing plays, and what else had he done?

Shakespeare's lost years are usually said to extend from 1585, when he disappears from the Stratford records, to 1592. I prefer to regard the period from 1564 to 1592 as 'lost'; for, excepting the three dates, 1582, 1583 and 1585, we have no certain knowledge of his activities or whereabouts during these twenty-eight years. About his father, John Shakespeare, we know a good deal; as for William, we assume that he went to Stratford's grammar school, that he did not go to university, and that he had commenced on his theatrical career some time before 1592, perhaps as early as 1586 or 1587. That still leaves many years to be accounted for; if William stayed at school till he was 15 or 16, when boys normally went to university,[1] the 'lost' years would be the period from 1579 to 1592. Did he begin his theatrical career much earlier than has been suspected? How else could he have passed these years? In the pages that follow I suggest that he worked for a while in Lancashire – a possibility explored by E. K. Chambers forty years ago, then rejected in 1970 by Douglas Hamer.

I shall return to Chambers and Hamer in a moment. First,

though, let us note that several early biographers and gatherers of memorabilia tell us about Shakespeare's career before he turned actor or dramatist. Some of their stories inspire little confidence – for example, John Aubrey's that 'his father was a butcher, and I have been told heretofore by some of the neighbours that when he was a boy he exercised his father's trade, but when he killed a calf he would do it in a high style and make a speech'. [2] Shakespeare's father appears several times in the Stratford records as a glover, [3] so we need not take the calf-killing too seriously. Two other stories, however, deserve more attention.

(1) 'His father, who was a considerable dealer in wool, had so large a family, ten children in all, that though he [William] was his eldest son, he could give him no better education than his own employment. He had bred him, 'tis true, for some time at a free-school ... ' (Rowe's *Life of Shakespeare,* 1709). Rowe's *Life* was partly based on hearsay supplied by Thomas Betterton, the actor, who had made a special journey to Stratford to collect whatever gossip he could. Might John Shakespeare have been a dealer in wool as a side-line? It now seems that he was, for three later discoveries have confirmed Rowe's story. (*a*) In the early nineteenth century, when the floors of John Shakespeare's house were taken up, 'the remains of wool, and the refuse of wool-combing, were found under the old flooring, embedded with the earth of the foundation'. (*b*) Leslie Hotson has uncovered a forgotten law-suit of 1599, in which John Shakespeare sued John Walford, a clothier, 'on a debt of £21; alleging that on November 4, 1568, at Stratford-on-Avon, Walford bought twenty-one tods of wool of him for £21'. (*c*) New information about John Shakespeare's illegal wool-dealing has come to light in the Public Record Office, and will be published shortly.[4] Rowe's story has been vindicated, so we have to accept that what Rowe tells us in the same breath – that William went to the 'free-school' (i.e. grammar school)[5] and worked for a while with his father – may be true as well.

(2) 'Though as Ben Jonson says of him, that he had but little Latin and less Greek, he understood Latin pretty well, for he had been in his younger years a schoolmaster in the country' (John Aubrey, *c.* 1681). This story seems to have a different ancestry from the one about calf-killing. Aubrey, an avid collector of biographical gossip, left a memorandum in his papers, 'quaere Mr Beeston who knows most of him from Mr Lacy; he lives in Shore-ditch at Hoglane.' Apparently the actor John Lacy had suggested that Aubrey should consult William Beeston, in Hog Lane; and the 'schoolmaster in the country' story, though written on the same page as 'his father was a

butcher ...', has a note in the margin, 'from Mr ... Beeston'. As others have observed, Aubrey's source is crucially important, for William Beeston (*c.* 1606–1682) was the son of Shakespeare's former colleague in the Lord Chamberlain's company, Christopher Beeston (died 1638), and was therefore in a position to know the facts.

In the absence of evidence to the contrary, we must be grateful for both of these statements as to Shakespeare's early career. William was the eldest son, and it is likely enough that his father (who owned or leased three houses in Stratford, also owned properties in Snitterfield and Wilmcote, and seems to have had extensive business interests) would want him in 'his own employment'. And the 'schoolmaster in the country' story, coming from William Beeston, is surely the best authenticated of all the early reports of Shakespeare's younger years. Our problem is not whether to believe it, but to know what to make of it. *Where* exactly, 'in the country'? If only we could narrow down this airy generalisation and give it a local habitation and a name – might this not be the key to unlock the mystery of the 'lost years'?

The search for William Shakespeare 'in the country' has yielded one important paper, 'William Shakeshafte', by E. K. Chambers (included in his *Shakespearean Gleanings* (Oxford, 1944)). Chambers here returned to the will of Alexander Hoghton, Esq., of Lea (in Lancashire), which he had already mentioned in *The Elizabethan Stage* and had then inexplicably overlooked while writing his monumental *William Shakespeare: A Study of Facts and Problems* (Oxford, 2 vols, 1930). Hoghton's will, dated 3 August 1581, and proved 12 September 1581, bequeathed his stock of play clothes and all his musical instruments to his brother Thomas, or, if he did not choose to keep players, to Sir Thomas Hesketh, and added 'And I most heartily require the said Sir Thomas to be friendly unto Fulk Gyllome and William Shakeshafte now dwelling with me and either to take them unto his service or else to help them to some good master, as my trust is he will'. The relevant passage (my transcription differs from that printed by Chambers in some details) will be found in Appendix A (p. 136). 'Was then William Shakeshafte a player in 1581?' Chambers wondered in 1923; and in 1944 he returned to this exciting possibility:

> The linking with Sir Thomas Hesketh seems to make it at least highly probable that Foke Gyllome and William Shakeshafte were players. The will goes on, firstly to provide for the payment of a year's wages to every servant of the testator at the time of his death, and secondly to recite a provision in an entail, dated on 20 July 1580, of his landed

property upon his brother Thomas, which reserved an annual rent-charge of £16 13s 4d to be spent in the provision of annuities for some of these servants .... There are eleven of them. One gets £3 6s 8d, four £1, two 13s 4d, and four £2. Among these last are William Shakeshafte and Fowke Gyllom, and also a Thomas Gyllome. There is a further direction that, on the death of any annuitant, his share is to be divided among those still living, so that the last survivor shall get for his life the whole amount of the rent charge (pp. 52–3).

Hoping that Hoghton's 'Shakeshafte' might turn out to be Shakespeare, Chambers listed several points that needed further investigation and hazarded some other suggestions. (1) The poet's grandfather, Richard, 'seems to be both Shakstaff and Shakeschafte, as well as Shakspere ... in the Snitterfield manor records'; 'it is at least conceivable that William might have adopted the variant as a player'. (2) We can learn 'a good deal about the Hoghton and Hesketh families' in *The Derby Household Books* (Chetham Society, xxxi, 1853), the record of weekly expenses of Henry, 4th Earl of Derby. (3) Sir Thomas Hesketh was related to Alexander Hoghton's wife, Elizabeth, she being a daughter of Gabriel Hesketh of Aughton, Lancashire. (4) When Sir Thomas Hesketh visited the Earl of Derby on 30 December 1587, the *Household Books* record 'On Saturday Sʳ Tho. Hesketh, Players went awaie'. 'I should like to be sure about that comma', Chambers added. 'Could he have written "Hesketh *and*" or "Hesketh*es*"?' (5) Chambers found an abstract of Hesketh's will, which 'contains no clear evidence that he maintained players'. (6) Probably Lord Derby's players, not heard of after 1582, 'passed to his son Ferdinando, Lord Strange'; when unnamed players performed at the Earl's houses, Chambers thought it 'possible that these anonymous players were Strange's own men'. (7) 'If William Shakeshafte passed from the service of Alexander Hoghton into that of either Thomas Hoghton or Sir Thomas Hesketh, he might very easily have gone on into that of Lord Strange, and so later into the London theatrical world.'

Chambers wrote this paper during the war, when some of the documents could not be inspected. In 1970 Douglas Hamer, having re-examined Hoghton's will, demolished several of Chambers's suggestions and concluded that 'it is now clear' that Shakespeare did not begin his dramatic career with the Hoghtons and the Heskeths. Hamer, I think, is right on some points and wrong on others; at the time, though, it was felt that he had effectively answered Chambers, and that the young Shakespeare's whereabouts 'in the country' must be sought elsewhere.

How, then, can we track down the elusive schoolmaster 'in the country'? Where do we start? It may seem a hopeless task, until we put the question differently (and apparently no one has done this) – namely, how does a gifted youth from provincial Stratford, without a university background or degree, find employment as a school-master? The obvious answer is that he must have been recommended as capable of the work of a schoolmaster, or an assistant master, even though he had no degree. Anyone in Stratford could have recommended him, but one person in particular would have been an invaluable referee: the schoolmaster at Stratford's grammar school, who would be able to give an expert opinion of young Shakespeare's scholarly attainments.

Although we have no documentary evidence to prove it biographers always assume that John Shakespeare, a well-to-do business-man in Stratford who in 1568 served as high bailiff (equivalent of the modern mayor), would send his son William to the town's grammar school. There is no good reason to suppose anything else – so we know the names of the schoolmasters who almost certainly taught William. In one case we know a good deal more than the name, and when we follow up the clues we are stopped short by a remarkable coincidence, to which I shall return in a moment.

William's first master was probably Walter Roche. In 1571 Simon Hunt succeeded him, but retired in 1575 to attend the Catholic seminary at Douay; he later became a Jesuit. Next in line was Thomas Jenkins, who had previously taught at Warwick grammar school. He was succeeded in 1579 by John Cottom, who remained until 1581 or 1582. 'By that time', says the entry in the *Shakespeare Encyclopaedia* (p. 197), 'Shakespeare had surely left the school. All these four masters were Oxford graduates and by the standards of the day, well-educated men.'

Checking through the information available about these four men, I was startled to learn that John Cottom was a native of Lancashire who returned *c.* 1582 to Tarnacre, where his family owned property, and lived there until his death in 1616. For Tarnacre, I found, is only ten miles from Lea, where the Hoghtons lived at this very time. Why had no one spotted this coincidence? The reason may be that T. W. Baldwin, following a suggestion by E. I. Fripp, demonstrated that Cottom came from Tarnacre in a book published in 1944, the very year of Chambers's essay on 'William Shakshafte'; John Cottom, it turns out, was the brother of the priest Thomas Cottam, who was captured by the authorities in June 1580, was arraigned on 14 November 1581, along with the Jesuit Edmund Campion, and executed as a traitor on 13 May 1582. Baldwin's proof that John Cottom, the Stratford schoolmaster, was the John Cottom of

Tarnacre, being one small detail embedded in the fact-crammed volumes of *William Shakspere's Small Latine and Lesse Greeke*,[6] was not seen to have importance, and was not connected with the 'Shakeshafte' theory propounded by Chambers in the same year.

Could William Shakeshafte, recommended by Alexander Hoghton in 1581, be William Shakespeare after all? Alerted by the closeness of Tarnacre to Lea, I began to search for further facts about John Cottom in the public archives, and discovered various connections between Alexander Hoghton and his family and John Cottom and *his* family — until it finally dawned on me that one of the many legatees under Alexander Hoghton's will, whose name appears as 'John Cotham' (cf. p. 137), may well be the teacher from Stratford. The 'schoolmaster' theory, it seems, leads straight back to Alexander Hoghton.

And so do many other friends and connections of Shakespeare in his later career. Alexander Hoghton belonged to an immensely wealthy and influential family, closely linked with other Lancashire families that play a part in Shakespeare's later life; the 'Lancashire connection' helps to illuminate people and events hitherto misunderstood or abandoned by biographers who were unable to fit together the jigsaw of Shakespeare's early life when so many pieces were missing. A good example is John Weever, an admirer who referred to Shakespeare in several works, the first being his *Epigrammes* (1599) with their verses *Ad Gulielmum Shakespeare*. The only modern reprint of this book is by one of the outstanding Elizabethan editors of our century, R. B. McKerrow (1911), who unfortunately chose to publish without much preliminary research. Weever had divided the *Epigrammes* into seven parts, or 'weeks', and had dedicated each week to a different man — Sir Richard Hoghton of Hoghton Tower; Robert Dalton of Pilling, Esq.; Sir Richard 'Mullineux'; Sir Edward Warren; Sir Thomas Gerard; Sir Cuthbert Halsey; Sir Peter Leigh. We cannot blame McKerrow for not drawing attention to the fact that Sir Richard Hoghton had inherited the estates of Alexander Hoghton of Lea (through Alexander's half-brother, Thomas Hoghton, Esq., Sir Richard's father), for Chambers had not yet explained the possible significance of Alexander Hoghton's bequest to 'Shakeshafte'; nevertheless, McKerrow should have looked into the family histories of Weever's dedicatees, which would have led to further discoveries about Weever (a neglected minor writer) and about Shakespeare. Dugdale's *The Baronage of England* would have informed him that Sir Richard Hoghton, Sir Richard Molyneux and Sir Peter Leigh had married three sisters, the daughters of Sir Gilbert Gerard, Queen Elizabeth's Master of the Rolls. Further research would have revealed that Weever's four other dedicatees were related to one or more of the three brothers-in-law through other family ties, or were associated with them in other ways; that other contemporaries addressed in Weever's individual epigrams were also related to the Hoghton circle; and that Weever himself was connected with the Hoghtons through his uncle, Henry Butler, Esq., a neighbour of John Cottom. Weever's *Epigrammes*, a collection more or less completed one year before it was published (i.e. in 1598), celebrates the family of its first and principal dedicatee, Sir Richard Hoghton, and, as I shall show, Weever's verses to Shakespeare signal to the informed reader that he is possessed of 'inside' information.

A second example of interconnecting threads that lead back to Lancashire involves the Stanley family and the Earls of Derby, whose *Household Books* so fortunately survive. Henry Stanley, the fourth Earl (c. 1531–1593), lived in almost regal style on his Lancashire estates; the Hoghtons and Heskeths and their relations appear frequently in the *Household Books* as visitors, and, as I shall argue, the case for Shakespeare's entering the London theatrical world as one of Derby's or Strange's Men is even stronger than Chambers suggested. In addition, the phoenix of Shakespeare's *The Phoenix and the Turtle* was almost certainly Ursula Halsall or Stanley, an illegitimate daughter of Henry Stanley, the fourth Earl; Ursula's sister, Dorothy, married (Sir) Cuthbert Halsall (or Halsey), one of the dedicatees of Weever's *Epigrammes*; and Sir Cuthbert, the phoenix's brother-in-law, was one of several Halsalls engaged in protracted legal battles with the Duddells of Salwick, one of whom was William Duddell, son-in-law of John Cottom, formerly schoolmaster at Stratford.

I have not attempted, in this introductory chapter, to list all the 'Lancashire' names that will interest future biographers of Shakespeare: many more will be found in the pages that follow. My aim has been to indicate that those who have written about Shakespeare's 'lost years' have missed important clues – which, I hope, will encourage us to look more searchingly at the relevant people and documents. And, first of all, at that fascinating family, the Hoghtons (or Houghtons) of Lea and Hoghton Tower.

# II

## Hoghton of Hoghton Tower

### (a) The early history of the Hoghton family

The Hoghtons are descended directly from Walter, one of the companions of
William the Conqueror, and through the female line from the Lady Godiva of
Coventry, wife of Leofric, Earl of Mercia. After the third generation from the
Norman Conquest, Adam de Hoghton first assumed the family name, holding
land in Hoghton in 1203. (*Guide to Hoghton Tower*)

Readers inclined to smile at the Hoghton family's claim to antiquity
would quickly mend their ways on opening the catalogues of
Hoghton muniments in the Lancashire Record Office, a vast collection of letters and legal documents of every kind, equally rich in the
medieval and Elizabethan and later periods.[1] If Shakespeare was
indeed a Hoghton retainer we should have little difficulty in recon-
structing his employer's family-history.

In the sixteenth century the Hoghtons were indisputably one of the
premier families in Lancashire. Sir Richard de Hoghton
(1498–1559), however, was succeeded by a son who became a
recusant (i.e. a Roman Catholic who refused to attend the services of
the Church of England) and left England in 1569, never to return: the
Right Worshipful Thomas Hoghton (1518–80) died in exile at Liège,
and could do little after 1569 to promote his family's fortune. Before
that, though, he had re-built Hoghton Tower (1562–8) on a ridge
about six miles south-east of Preston – a magnificent baronial
residence, with upper and base courts, so large, it has been said, that
it 'appears at a distance almost like a fortified town'. The tower itself
was blown up during the civil war, but was described by Richard
Kuerden in the seventeenth century as 'a most princely tower ... a
very tall strong tower or gate-house', 'a stately fabric ... environed
with a most spacious park'.[2] Thomas's son, a priest, was debarred
from the succession, so the next head of the family was Thomas's
brother, Alexander, who died next year (1581) and recommended
William Shakeshafte in his will to his half-brother, another Thomas,

[8]

who now succeeded him. This Thomas died in a night-skirmish in 1589, and was followed by his son, Richard (1570–1630), who was knighted in 1599 and became the first baronet in 1611. A family tree will be found in Appendix B, p. 146.

Seekers of the 'schoolmaster in the country' will be particularly interested in Alexander and Thomas Hoghton, but we must begin with Thomas the exile, whom I shall call Thomas I. The whole family appears to have remained ardently Catholic until Richard Hoghton turned Protestant, probably in the 1580s. (According to Dugdale, Richard Hoghton and his brothers-in-law, who married the daughters of Sir Gilbert Gerard, the Master of the Rolls (cf. p. 6), had all 'formerly been in Ward to him [Sir Gilbert], as I have credibly heard': it is believed that Sir Gilbert saw to it that his future sons-in-law turned Protestant.[3]) Thomas I, being a recusant, took elaborate precautions to safeguard the family's inheritance, which can be traced in various deeds and conveyances from near the beginning of Elizabeth's reign; he listed his father's sons and illegitimate sons as his heirs,[4] and conveyed some properties to faithful family retainers, one of whom (George Beseley) reappears later as one of the executors of Alexander Hoghton's will in 1581. Having made over messuages etc. to 'Georgio Besely de Gosenarghe generoso' (i.e. George Beseley of Goosnargh, gentleman) and another, he explained that 'the intent of this deed is that the said George and Roger shall stand seized of the premises ... unto the use of the said Thomas Hoghton and his heirs male'.[5] Two of Alexander Hoghton's executors in 1581, George Beseley and James Helme, were involved in a similar legal manoeuvre in 1585: a damaged seventeenth-century copy of an indenture dated 27 Elizabeth (i.e. 1585) records an agreement between Thomas Hoghton of Hoghton (Alexander's heir) and George Beasley and James Belme, but *Bretton v. Adam Hoghton* (2 James I) referred back to this indenture and correctly named the two men as Besely and 'James Helme'.[6] Other recusant families protected their interests in similar ways; in the case of the Hoghtons, the resulting legal documents help us to disentangle some of the mysteries of Alexander's will of 1581.

The Catholic sympathies of the older Hoghtons (including Alexander) are important for us, since it is highly unlikely that such a family would employ, at a time so dangerous for recusants, a servant who was not a practising Catholic. The phrasing of Shakespeare's will suggests that he died a Protestant, but there are reasons for believing that his father and daughter, Susanna, may have been Catholics (cf. p. 116). If the dramatist changed his religion in his teens or later — as did John Donne, Ben Jonson and many more — this would certainly interest readers of *King John* and *Hamlet* (to name only two of the plays concerned with anti-papal propaganda and/or Catholic ideas). I return to the Shakespeares later (p. 114 ff.), and, at this stage, merely outline some of the basic facts about the Hoghtons and *their* religion. As good a starting-point as any is the ballad, 'The Blessed Conscience', celebrating Thomas I and his honourable decision that religion comes before worldly profit. It is popularly ascribed to Roger Anderton, Thomas's butler, who went into exile with his master, and it seems to be based on detailed knowledge of Thomas's affairs. Much of the ballad (it consists of twenty-three eight-line stanzas) purports to give Thomas's own dying words.[7]

> At Hoghton, where I used to rest
> Of men I had great store,
> Full twenty gentlemen at least,
> Of yeomen good three score!
> And of them all, I brought but two
> With me, when I came thence.
> I left them all ye world knows how
> To keep my conscience!

It was clearly a difficult time, for 'I durst not trust my dearest friend, / But secretly stole hence'. And even Thomas's brothers, he thought, let him down.

> When to my brethren I had sent
> Ye welcome that they made
> Was false reports me to present,
> Which made my conscience sad.
> My brethren all did thus me cross
> And little regard my fall,
> Save only one, that rued my loss,
> That is Richard, of Park Hall.
>
> He was ye comfort that I had;
> I proved his diligence;
> He was as just as they were bad,
> Which cheered my consciènce. ...

Richard Hoghton of Park Hall, in Charnock Richard, 'was the son of Sir Richard Hoghton by his fourth wife, Anne, daughter of Roger Browne, though he was born out of wedlock'.[8] By great good fortune, the letters sent by Thomas I to his brother Richard survive in the John Rylands Library, Manchester (English MSS. 213). They begin on 22 September 1576, and continue at regular (sometimes weekly) intervals, with many references to Hoghton retainers who travelled to and from the continent carrying money and messages. Richard Hoghton clearly acted as 'business manager' for his exiled brother, and may have been the most committed Catholic of the 'brethren' who remained in England: when Edmund Campion was captured by the authorities in 1581 it was reported that the Jesuit had stayed with leading Catholics in Lancashire, whose houses were searched by order of the Privy Council – 'and especially the house of Richard Hoghton, where it is said the said Campion left his books'.[9] Examined upon his oath 'whether the said Campion had ever to his knowledge been in his house', Richard Hoghton 'deposed the contrary', and witnesses deposed that Hoghton was 'conformable in religion' i.e. attended the Anglican church; however, many Catholics 'conformed outwardly', and deposed falsely about their religion; Richard's role as 'manager' for Thomas I, and other contemporary evidence (cf. p. 20), make it likely that he was a Catholic.

Let us return to Thomas I, the head of the family until 1580. His importance (and consequently Alexander's, when he succeeded as head of the family) can be illustrated from many sources. Thomas's unlicensed departure from the country was reported to the Privy Council (29 September 1571), and shortly afterwards a Special Commission was ordered to report on his possessions and tenants.[10] In 1576 the Queen signed a licence permitting Richard Hoghton to travel to Antwerp 'to the intent to advise, persuade and counsel Thomas Hoghton, late of Hoghton, ... to return unto this our realm', two sureties being 'bound' with Richard to lose £200 if Richard failed to come back within two months.[11] The government looked upon Thomas I as a person of considerable importance. So did the Catholic church, for the future Cardinal Allen attended the opening of Hoghton Tower when Thomas I had re-built and extended the family's old home, and shortly after Thomas's death the Cardinal wrote that he had received £100 from Thomas's executors for the benefit 'of the church at Preston, when the time should serve'. And a handsome monument was erected for Thomas I in the church of Gervais, Liège, where he was buried, with the following inscription: 'Hic e regione sepultus est vir Illustris D. Thomas Hoghton, Anglus, qui post decem an. exilium spontaneum variasque patrimonii et rerum omnium direptiones propter Cath. fidei confessionem a sectariis illatas, obijt 4 Non. Jun. 1580. Ætat. 63'.[12]

Precisely how the 'bad' brethren of Thomas I managed to 'cross' him may never be fully known. The ballad alleges that his brothers offered a thousand marks (i.e. £666 13s 4d) 'to hinder my licence / That I should not come home again'; my own guess is that they felt they had to protect themselves, and perhaps refused to surrender legal documents that were needed by Thomas I – a common dilemma in recusant families, whose properties might be confiscated by the crown. Something of the sort may lie behind the complaint of Brian Jackson (the principal messenger between Thomas I and Richard Hoghton in the 1570s) and others to the Privy Council (1 March 1581) 'against Alexander Hoghton of Hoghton, Esq., and others his brethren, for the detaining of sundry leases and annuities given heretofore unto the plaintiffs by Thomas Hoghton, their oldest brother deceased, in consideration of eighteen years' service'.[13] The Hoghtons had to contend with many problems in the 1570s and 1580s, which we need to know about to understand Alexander's will of 1581 and the flurry of legal activity that preceded and followed it; and it may be that they were a divided family, which would increase their anxieties. Catholic families were not necessarily held together by their fear of Queen Elizabeth's Protestant government. Alexander's widow,to give one more example, thought that two men whom he had asked in his will to be his executor and supervisor behaved disgracefully towards her; they happened to be her own brothers – but that is another family and another story, and must wait till later.

Alexander survived as head of the family for just over a year (1580–1). I shall look more closely at his will, and his household and circle of friends, in the next two sections, and continue here with a brief account of Alexander's brother and heir, Thomas II (died 1589), and his son and heir, Richard. Many records survive about both men, from which I select a few of the more interesting ones. Thomas II, in the lifetime of Thomas I and Alexander Hoghton, 'did occupy ... one messuage or tenement called the Brynscowes' and received the rents of divers other lands in 'Whelton [i.e. Wheelton] and Withnell' (DL4.29.39: deposition of Richard Hoghton of Park Hall, 29 Eliz.). On 19 August 1581, Thomas II made an agreement with 'Elizabeth Hoghton, widow, late wife of Alexander Hoghton, Esq.', conveying to her 'Alston Hall and all lands late the inheritance of Thomas Hoghton, Esq.' (BL: Add. MS. 32, 106, fo. 165b).[14] In 27 Elizabeth (1585), Thomas II made an indenture 'for the preferment of William, Thomas and Adam Hoghton, his younger sons' (*ibid.*, fo. 223), leaving them lands in Hoghton, Lea, Withnell, etc. In 1588 he paid the Crown £100 for the defence of the realm (DDF 2440, fo. 20b). On 16 September 1589, he signed a receipt for £300 to Sir Gilbert Gerard 'due unto me the said Thomas Hoghton this present day, being the day of the marriage of Richard Hoghton my son unto Katherine Gerard, daughter of the said Sir Gilbert Gerard' (DDHo 345). Throughout this decade Thomas II also battled with Ann Halsall, the grandmother of Sir Cuthbert Halsall (cf. p. 53), over rights of pasturage, turbary, etc., in Lea and in adjacent lands; witnessed a bill of complaint of 1582, a decree of 1584, interrogatories of 1585, etc.[15] These disputes are probably connected with Thomas's death on 20 November 1589, when Thomas Langton, baron of Newton, with about eighty armed men, attacked Thomas Hoghton's house at midnight, ostensibly in a dispute about cattle; Hoghton had thirty men to defend him, but was killed in the melee. It was, it seems, a dark night; the Langton party used the watch-word 'The crow is white!', and Hoghton's men cried 'Black, black!'

The Earl of Derby reported to the Privy Council on 10 December that he had taken great pains to investigate this riot, in which several leading Lancashire families were involved,[16] and the Queen herself sent a most unusual letter to the justices at Lancaster. (The manuscript contains so many deletions and insertions that I quote from the *Calendar* summary of State Papers Domestic.)

> The Queen to Justices Clinch and Walmsley. Understands that Justice Walmsley, contrary to her express commands, signified by a letter from the late Lord Chancellor, has bailed sundry persons indicted of the murder of Thos. Houghton, of Lancashire; wonders how he dared to presume so far, showing both contempt of her commandment, and little regard for the due administration of justice. ... Commands him to cause the said parties to be immediately returned to prison, and to proceed ... to a speedy trial without further bail, and not to fail at his peril.[17]

In the much-corrected original we find the Queen's personal concern even more strongly expressed: the Lord Chancellor's letter was 'written by our order' (interlined); and the letter ends 'as you will avoid our furder indignation, and answer for the contrary at your peril'. Lord Strange, the Earl of Derby's heir (and probably Shakespeare's patron at this time), attended the spring assizes in Lancaster in April 1590, and stayed a whole week on account of the baron of Newton's trial.[18] In the end the baron made his peace with the Hoghtons by ceding to them the manor of Walton le Dale.

According to the 'valor and extent of the estate inherited by Richard Hoghton', dated 1590, the manors of Hoghton and Lea descended from Thomas II to his son Richard. These encompassed 800 messuages, 400 cottages, 20 water mills, 10 wind mills, 1000 gardens, 1000 orchards, 2000 acres of meadow, 3000 acres of pasture, 2000 acres of woodlands, 6000 acres of land, 6000 acres of moor, 1000 acres of turbary and 1000 acres of heath.[19] Round numbers, it will be noticed, and they need to be compared with the inquisition post mortem in the Public Record Office (DL7. 15.39), where the names of Hoghton tenants are listed, and the rents they paid. Without going into detail we can see that the family was immensely wealthy, and that Mrs Anne Hoghton (the widow of Thomas II) might indeed have been able to live at the rate of £1,000 a year, as rumour reported.[20]

The most eventful year in Richard Hoghton's life was 1598–9, when he became High Sheriff of Lancashire. It was perhaps because he served as Sheriff that, as John Chamberlain wrote on 28 June 1599, he was knighted on Sunday at court.[21] Sometime in the next five months John Weever dedicated his *Epigrammes* to 'Sir Richard Hoghton of Hoghton Tower, Justice of Peace, and Quorum; High Sheriff of Lancashire, etc.', and mentioned 'the experience which many scholars have had of your kindness, never to be forgotten'. Sir Richard, particularly in his year as Sheriff, proved a notable hunter of recusants, and reported his catches to the Bishop of Chester and to Sir Robert Cecil;[22] the Bishop wrote to Cecil in October 1600 that Sir Richard and his successor as Sheriff 'have done great service in apprehending of sundry priests, pestilent persuaders to rebellion, and are the ablest and fittest persons ... to hunt out the seditious priests'.[23] A few days earlier Sir Richard informed Cecil that he had caught a seminary priest, one who 'seems a very mean scholar' (*SPD*, 1 Oct. 1600), which may mean that Sir Richard was something of a scholar (cf. Weever, above). What would the older Hoghtons have thought of these activities?

Sir Richard, of course, appears in the official records of the period as Sheriff or J.P., and also in many legal documents. In 1593, when Sir Richard Molyneux made out a deed of gift for his wife (since she 'hath no jointure'), his brothers-in-law figure as sureties – Sir Thomas Gerard, and Peter Legh and Richard Hoghton, Esquires (DDCl.910); as his friend Sir Cuthbert Halsall sank more and more into debt, Sir Richard Hoghton helped him as security:[24] all these men, it will be recalled, receive dedications in Weever's *Epigrammes*. Richard's widowed mother continued to live at Lea Hall, where Alexander and Thomas II had died, even after she married Richard Sherburne, Esq.; in her will (9 James I) she asked to be buried near her former husband, Thomas Hoghton.

Weever referred to the splendour of Sir Richard's principal residence, the 'gold-gilded tower' (sig. F6). In August 1617 James I and his court visited Hoghton Tower, and stayed three days. Harrison Ainsworth gave a detailed account of this visit in Book III ('Hoghton Tower') of *The Lancashire Witches* (1848), a romance partly based on contemporary records. The king inspected Sir Richard's alum mines, and later asked the Lord Chancellor and Lord Treasurer to advise him whether or not to take over these mines, as

Sir Richard requested. (Sir Richard had mortgaged the manor of Walton to finance the mines, which seem to have been a bad speculation; 'towards the end of his life', said G. C. Miller, 'Sir Richard was for some years imprisoned for debt in the Fleet'[25].) Sir Richard's son, Gilbert (born 1591) had been knighted in 1606, at an unusually early age, and Sir Richard himself was elevated to the Baronetage in 1611.

Hasler's account of Sir Richard Hoghton in *The House of Commons 1558–1603* differs from mine in several respects. It states that Thomas I was the father of Thomas II and grandfather of Sir Richard; and that Richard Hoghton was married *c.* 1590 and knighted in 1598.

## (b) Alexander Hoghton's will (1581) and 'Shakeshafte'

We are now ready to go back to Alexander Hoghton of Lea, and to ask whether he was eliminated prematurely from our search for the 'schoolmaster in the country'. Since John Cottom, a Stratford schoolmaster in 1579 when Shakespeare was 15, belonged to a family with property so close to Alexander Hoghton's house, and since John Cottom actually lived at Tarnacre from *c.* 1582, we must re-open the case of 'William Shakeshafte'. What, in the first place, made Douglas Hamer so certain in 1970 that Shakespeare did not work for the Hoghtons and Heskeths? I begin with a summary of Hamer's argument.[26]

(1) 'If he actually were employed in far-off Lancashire under an alias in and before 1581, it is strange that, reverting to his paternal and baptismal name of Shakespeare, he should ... marry Anne Hathaway in 1582, live continuously in Stratford until after the birth of his twins in 1585, and then ... reappear in 1587 as a "player" ... in the service of Sir Thomas Hesketh in Lancashire'. (2) Hamer also showed 'Shakeshafte' to be a not uncommon name in the Preston Burgess Rolls (Preston was close to Alexander Hoghton's house at Lea), and published, among others, an entry for 1582: 'Johannes Shakeshafte Glover Juratus / Willelmus Shakeshafte frater eius Juratus / Willelmus Shakeshafte filius eius'. (3) He contended that Hoghton's bequest of annuities to eleven servants, including Fulke Gyllom and William Shakeshafte, amounts to 'an early non-subscription form of the Tontine system – survivor takes all'.

[Since] the annuitants draw annuities which increase with the death of each annuitant until the last draws the whole income for life, the annuitants are initially graded according to their actual ages at the time when the capital sum or capital income is established. The basic idea is that over the years all the annuitants shall, in the normal way of living and dying, receive approximately the same amount. The oldest annuitant thus receives the highest initial annuity.

William Shakeshafte was one of four legatees who received £2 each; only one of the thirty named legatees (cf. p. 137) received more; therefore, said Hamer, the inescapable deduction is that Shakeshafte 'may have been as old as thirty to forty'. William Shakespeare of Stratford, on the other hand, was only seventeen in 1581. (4) Chambers assumed that the players referred to in Hoghton's will must be actors. The straightforward interpretation of this passage in the will (see p. 136), thought Hamer, 'is that the musical instruments, play-clothes, and players all go together, and that here we have to do, not with musical instruments and actors, but with musical instruments and musicians'. The term *player* had been current since 1463 to signify 'One who plays an instrument of music' (*OED*); *play-clothes* 'are not recorded in *OED*'. (5) Two years after publishing 'William Shakeshafte', Chambers announced that 'Sir Thomas Hesketh had in fact players in 1587';[27] this was partly because he now knew that in the printed version of *The Derby Household Books*, the entry 'Sir Thomas Hesketh, Players went awaie' has a comma added by the editor. Hamer, however, observed that the *Household Books* 'invariably used the terminal -s of the possessive' (i.e. 'Hesketh' is not a possessive); and that, comparing this Hesketh entry with others recording comings and goings at the earl's houses, it most probably means 'Sir Thomas Hesketh came, and the players went away'.

As already indicated, I disagree with several of Hamer's arguments. I shall comment first on (3), which, if correct, would put an end to all further discussion. A legal colleague, Professor D. W. Elliott, advised me some years ago that Alexander Hoghton's provisions in his will should not be seen as an early non-subscription tontine.

> I guess that each annuitant enjoyed his annuity for life, it then went to the survivors, who enjoyed augmented annuities for their lives, and then to the last survivor, who enjoyed a large annuity but only for the remainder of his life. The capital then reverted to the testator's estate. A tontine was quite different; it was an early form of life insurance, very crude and with a strong element of gambling. No participant enjoyed anything unless and until he became the last survivor, when he took the whole capital absolutely. In other words, annuities played no part in the scheme at all …
>
> Nor do I think it at all credible to deduce the age of the annuitants from the comparative size of the annuities given to them. I take it the

argument is that an old servant has not long to live, and will not enjoy accretions by survival, so must be given more than a young servant. Perhaps, but other deductions from a large gift are: satisfaction with the servant, long service by the servant, status of the servant ... other resources of the servant ... It is the way of the world to reward long and faithful service, but there has never been any 'practice' to do so. I would be most unconvinced by any reconstruction of servants' comparative ages from their comparative bequests.[28]

Professor Elliott pretty well disposes of Hamer's tontine argument. And, in case any doubts remain, I can now give some additional information: several of Hoghton's annuitants appeared as deponents in later law-suits, identifying themselves and stating their age. We can therefore work out how old they were in 1581: and the figures do not bear out Hamer's argument.

(*a*) *Thomas Barton* was Alexander Hoghton's steward. Lawrence Fydler of Lea deposed in 1605 that he was 'three several times sent unto the now complainant by Mr Alexander Hoghton and Thomas Barton, gent., then steward to the said Mr Alexander Hoghton for to come to agree with Mr Hoghton for a lease' (*Bretton v. Adam Hoghton*, DL4.48.49). Barton described himself in 1587 as 'Thomas Barton, gentleman and servant to Thomas Hoghton, Esq.', aged about fifty, and referred to Alexander Hoghton as 'his late master' (*Mary Lyvesey v. Thomas Hoghton*, DL4.29.39). Barton, therefore, was 44 or so in 1581.

(*b*), (*c*) *Thomas Coston* and *Henry 'Bonnde'* are deponents in *Singleton v. R. Hoghton*, 1586 (DL4.28.25). Coston gives his age as 34, Bond his as 60. Coston states that Thomas Hoghton I used to send him 'into England divers and sundry times yearly to the said Richard Hoghton to receive money of him to his use'. Richard Hoghton, of Park Hall in Charnock Richard, Thomas's 'base brother', managed his estates for him in his absence (cf. p. 10) and, as we learn from Henry Bond in the same suit, delivered the rents to George Hoghton or Brian Jackson or Thomas Coston. No doubt the Thomas 'Costin' named as one of Thomas Hoghton's defenders in the Earl of Derby's report on the 'affray' of 1589[29] was the same faithful family retainer. Coston would have been 29 and Bond 55 in 1581.

For our immediate purposes these three names suffice. Thomas Barton, aged 44 in 1581, would have to be one of the younger annuitants according to Hamer's theory, since he was left no specified sum; Bond, aged 55, would also have to be one of the younger annuitants, for the same reason; and Coston would have to be older than either Barton or Bond, since he was left an annuity of £1 a year; yet Coston was in fact younger. Hamer's argument (3) collapses.

We have still to consider Hamer's other arguments. Let us begin with (1) and (2): it seems to me misleading to think of Shakespeare's switching to 'Shakeshafte', if this happened, as going 'under an alias'. Names simply were not thought of as fixed and unalterable in the sixteenth century: Marlowe is also Marley, Morley and Marlin in contemporary records; Philip Henslowe is also Hinslye, Hinshow, Henshlowe, Henseslowe; Shakespeare, even when famous, appears in the Revels accounts as Shaxberd,[30] and his grandfather, Richard, figures in the Snitterfield records as 'Shakstaff' (but not as 'Shakeshafte', as Chambers thought);[31] and the only other Snitterfield Shakespeare, Thomas, is also 'Shakesmore' in 1578.[32] In Lancashire the familiar name was Shakeshafte, and so it would not be surprising if a name as unusual (in this area) as Shakespeare were assimilated, or perhaps merely confused by the scrivener in 1581.

As for Hamer's (4) and (5), a weakness in his case is that he can cite no example of *play-clothes* meaning 'the official costumes of musicians'. I believe, as he does, that Hoghton's *instruments, play-clothes* and *players* go together, but not that instruments point exclusively to a band of musicians. Richard Jones's deed of sale of 1589, making over to Edward Alleyn his share 'of playing apparel, play-books, instruments and other commodities'[33] helps to explain: actors at this time had to be all-purpose entertainers, acrobats and musicians as well as *histriones*. Quite a number of Shakespeare's colleagues were definitely singers or instrumentalists; Henslowe's players spent large sums to buy apparel and instruments – these being the indispensable tools of their trade. In the very year of Hoghton's will, 1581, 'certain companies of players' petitioned the Privy Council for a licence to perform publicly, since they 'were only brought up from their youth in the practice of music and playing', and this was granted because the plague had abated and 'they are to present certain plays before the Queen's Majesty'.[34] Unless an example turns up of *play-clothes* meaning musicians' clothes, the natural interpretation of Hoghton's bequest must be that he kept a group of 'players' who produced plays, or who made music and sometimes produced plays. (At least some of the boy-actors in Shakespeare's company were trained singers; his colleague Augustine Phillips, who bequeathed musical instruments to his 'apprentices', had clearly taken an interest in their musical skills; another colleague, R. Cowley, took a musician's part in *Seven Deadly Sins*, and another, R. Armin, was called on to sing in several plays. See also *Henslowe's Diary*, pp. 102, 122 etc., for the purchase of instruments.)

The actual phrasing of Alexander Hoghton's will contradicts

Hamer's interpretation of *play-clothes*. Why would Alexander describe them as 'all my instruments belonging to musics *and all manner of play-clothes*' except to imply the diversity of these garments? If Alexander had in mind some sort of uniform worn by the musicians, or his own livery, as Hamer suggested, why *all manner of*? This phrase surely points to a stock of costumes kept for theatrical entertainments by Alexander's players. And, though Hamer is probably right in claiming that *The Derby Household Books* do not prove the existence of 'Sir Thomas Hesketh's players',[35] the really important point is that Alexander Hoghton, though uncertain whether or not his brother would want to keep players, ordained that if Thomas II declined then Sir Thomas Hesketh 'shall have' the instruments and play-clothes; that is, he knew that Hesketh would take them, presumably because Hesketh kept players. Moreover, as Chambers saw, although Gyllom and Shakeshafte are not positively identified as players in Hoghton's will, 'the linking with Sir Thomas Hesketh seems to make it at least highly probable'.

This last point is placed in a new perspective when one compares the printed version of Alexander Hoghton's will with the manuscript in the Lancashire Record Office. The nineteenth-century editor omitted some of the meaningless phrases of the will, and also the word 'Itm' (Item), which is used to introduce the testator's different bequests. For our purposes it is crucial that a single 'Itm' covers three related matters: (1) the instruments and play-clothes are left to Thomas II, if he will keep players; (2) they go to Sir Thomas Hesketh, if Thomas II declines; (3) Sir Thomas is asked to employ Gyllom and Shakeshafte, or 'to help them to some good master'. In this three-part bequest Alexander Hoghton is concerned with his players and their future, and it follows that Gyllom and Shakeshafte are mentioned after (1) and (2) because they are connected in his mind with his players.

How does all this help us in our search for the 'schoolmaster in the country'? As already stated, I believe that William Shakespeare could have been recommended to Alexander Hoghton by John Cottom, the master of Stratford's grammar school. Schoolmasters, of course, had to be officially licensed at this time, but Catholic families, as well as illegally harbouring priests, frequently maintained unlicensed schoolmasters; and this was particularly common in Lancashire. Indeed, a report to the Privy Council 'on the condition of Lancashire and Cheshire' of *c*. 1591 complained that even licensed school-masters were 'unsound': 'small reformation has been made there by the Ecclesiastical Commission, as may appear by the emptiness of churches on Sundays ... The youth are for the most part trained up by such as profess papistry; no examination is had of schools and schoolmasters'.[36] Young William Shakespeare could have gone to Lancashire as an assistant teacher in 1579 or 1580, when he was fifteen or sixteen, and, like the master of the Children of Paul's and of the Children of the Chapel, could have been drawn into 'theatricals' in the course of his normal duties.

Apart from Alexander Hoghton's concern for William Shake-shafte in 1581, and other Hoghton–Shakespeare links that will emerge presently, there are good reasons for pursuing what may at first seem a far-fetched hypothesis. (1) John Shakespeare, William's father, began to experience financial difficulties from about 1577. He mortgaged a house and land, and at the same time stopped attending regularly at the Stratford council's meetings. Whatever his problems, his financial future must have looked less secure than formerly; if William was reluctant to help his father 'in his own employment' (cf. p. 2), this would have been his opportunity to break away. (2) Other precocious boys of sixteen or so have worked as teachers. Richard Mather (1596–1669), later one of the most celebrated New England Puritans, began to teach at a grammar school in Lancashire at the age of fifteen; Simon Forman, still in his teens, taught as an unqualified usher from 1572; and, in a later period, Mrs Gaskell records that Patrick Bronte, the father of the Bronte sisters, 'opened a public school at the early age of sixteen', and taught for five or six years.[37] Others have done it, so why not Shakespeare? (3) Other members of the Hoghton family, and other Catholics closely connected with the family, reputedly maintained unlicensed schoolmasters at this very time. An apostate priest informed Lord Burghley in 1592 that Richard Hoghton of Park Hall (cf. p. 10) 'hath kept a recusant schoolmaster I think this twenty years. He hath had one after another; the name of one was Scholes, of the other Fawcett, as I remember, but I stand in doubt of the names'. The same informer claimed that Mrs Anne Hoghton, the widow of Thomas II, kept at her house in Lea 'Richard Blundell, brother to William Blundell, of Crosbie, gent., an obstinate papist', to teach her children to sing and play on the virginals; and that Mr Bartholomew Hesketh (the brother of Alexander Hoghton's widow) 'had kept for sundry years a certain Gabriel Shaw to be his school-master'; and that William Hulton of Hulton, Esq., a close friend of the Hoghtons, had kept a recusant school-master 'many years.[38] (Hulton is named in an indenture, 30 Elizabeth, with Thomas Hoghton, Esq., and Sir Richard Molyneux, as surety for the jointure of Anne Hoghton, Thomas's wife; and Hulton and his two sons tracked down the testament's 'source'. James G. McManaway established in 1967 that the testament is an English version of Carlo Borromeo's *Testament of the Soul*, a standardised 'spiritual testament' signed by Catholics as a profession of faith; Borromeo died in 1585, and his formulary was translated and dispersed by the thousand. A Spanish version printed in 1661 in Mexico City and an English one dated 1638 have now resurfaced – and if Malone came across such a document without knowing that it reprinted a much earlier text, he would naturally assume that Jordan or another had forged the testament by copying from a booklet printed after John Shakespeare's death. But that inference can no longer stand, and the belated proof that the testament conformed with Catholic practice, instead of being an eccentric, self-incriminating gesture by John Shakespeare, suggests that it must have been genuine.[16]

John Shakespeare's Spiritual Testament, as printed by Malone, consists of fourteen sections, and very closely corresponds to the English version of Borromeo printed in 1638. Here is a specimen, the beginning of section X: 'Item, I John Shakspear do protest, that I am willing, yea, I do infinitely desire and humbly crave, that of this my last will and testament the glorious and ever Virgin Mary, mother of God, refuge and advocate of sinners, (whom I honour specially above all other saints,) may be the chief Executress, together with these other saints, my patrons, (saint Winefride) all whom I invoke and beseech to be present at the hour of my death ... ' Since the original has disappeared we do not know whether John Shakespeare wrote out the complete text or simply inserted his name and patron saint etc. wherever the document left blanks to be filled in.

The Testament remained in private hands and no one sought to profit by it from 1757 until 1784 (when Jordan borrowed and copied it, with a view to publication). Although it has disappeared, there is no good reason for impugning its authenticity, or for doubting that William Shakespeare was brought up by a father who, like so many of his generation, continued in the Old Faith. Returning now to the two explanations of John Shakespeare's puzzling career from *c.* 1577 (cf. p. 115), we may ask whether they are mutually exclusive, as is normally assumed. John must have had cash-flow problems, or else he would not have sold so much property; at the same time he would have found it convenient, if a Catholic, to plead fear of 'process for debt', and thus to avoid church-going. Let us remember that 'he never became poor. He was never forced to part with the three houses he owned in Stratford';[17] and the two fines of £20 that he had to pay in 1580 would not have been imposed on a beggar. His withdrawal from the 'halls' or meetings of Stratford's Corporation is best explained as connected with the Corporation's responsibility for church affairs: since the Corporation fined Stratfordians for profanity and for non-attendance at church, a Catholic John Shakespeare would have been most uncomfortable helping to persecute his co-religionists. His retiring from the 'halls' as the government's hostility to Catholics increased, even though he was still a substantial property-owner in 1577–80, taken together with his Spiritual Testament, drives us to the conclusion that the dramatist's father was a Catholic.[18]

A forthcoming paper on 'John Shakespeare in the Exchequer', by D. L. Thomas and N. E. Evans of the Public Record Office, significantly changes our picture of the dramatist's father, and supports the view that he is unlikely to have withdrawn from Corporation business for financial reasons. Thomas and Evans have discovered that John Shakespeare faced four prosecutions in the Exchequer, in the 1570s, for usury and illegal wool dealing. One alleged that John Shakespeare, of Stratford upon Avon, glover, had lent £100 at 20 per cent; another, that he lent £80 at 20 per cent. (Usury at 10 per cent was permitted at certain times in the sixteenth century.) John was also accused of buying 200 tods of wool (5,600 pounds) with another purchaser, and 100 tods on his own. Large sums of money were involved; and, even though John paid a £2 fine in one case, and probably similar fines in others, it now appears that he was a much wealthier man than has been assumed. The theory that he ran into serious financial difficulties in 1577 (when he stopped attending 'halls', while still possessed of many properties that were only disposed of later) becomes more implausible the more we learn about the full range of his business dealings. In fact, we now know so much more about John Shakespeare than did nineteenth-century biographers that it is high time to challenge the much-repeated statement that John Shakespeare could not have been worth £500 in 1596, as was claimed when he applied for a grant of arms,[19] unless William's assets were included with John's; on the contrary, William may well have got rich so quickly because he was given a helping hand by a wealthy father.

To return to our starting-point: William, we have reason to believe, was brought up as a Catholic. And if William also served Alexander Hoghton and Sir Thomas Hesketh, two very positively committed Catholics, how can we reconcile this with the anti-Catholic tone of some of his early plays? We may do so by examining the career of his patron from c. 1586 (as I have argued, p. 59 ff.), viz. of Ferdinando Stanley, Lord Strange, and of Ferdinando's father, the fourth Earl of Derby. The Earl officiated as President at the trial of Mary, Queen of Scots, and as Lord High Steward at the trial of the Earl of Arundel, eldest son of the Duke of Norfolk, who was arraigned on a charge of high treason in 1589; his family, however, included an embarrassing number of known or suspected Catholics: 'Lady Margaret Clifford [his wife] from whom he was separated was a Catholic – as was also his brother, Thomas Stanley of Winwick. His sisters, daughters of his devout stepmother, Margaret, Countess of Derby, née Barlow, were Catholics also, as were his brothers-in-law, Lords Stafford and Morley, Sir John Arundell and Sir Nicholas Pointz.'[20] The Earl, we may suppose, persecuted recusants partly because he felt he had to prove himself. As we have recently learned, some Lancashire Protestants wanted the Earl to act much more positively against Catholics. 'Resentment flared into clashes between a Protestant ginger group and the earl of Derby and his fellow members of the ecclesiastical commission. In 1587 the most vociferous spokesman of the Protestant group, Edward Fleetwood, indicted the earl for being too lax and he urged Burghley to carry out a purge of the commission.'[21] Lord Strange, commended by the Privy Coucil in 1587 for his diligence against recusants,[22] no doubt felt equally incriminated by his family and by his Catholic friends in Lancashire: when he was approached by the Jesuits in 1593 to claim the crown in succession to Queen Elizabeth (cf. p. 37) he could hardly have been surprised to learn that government spies were closely watching him. In such an atmosphere of general suspicion the Earl and Lord Strange needed to demonstrate their loyalty, and Lord Strange's Men could help by producing plays with an unmistakable anti-Catholic bias.

Shakespeare's first flights in anti-Catholic propaganda are to be found in Parts 1 and 2 of *Henry VI* (c. 1588–9). The feeling of these plays irresistibly supports 'good Duke Humphry', the Lord Protector, against the arrogance of that 'scarlet hypocrite', Cardinal Beaufort, the Bishop of Winchester. 'Thou that giv'st whores indulgences to sin', the Duke tells the Bishop –

> Under my feet I stamp thy cardinal's hat,
> In spite of Pope or dignities of church.
>
> (*I Henry VI*, I.3)

Here the feeling is largely directed against an individual, rather than against Rome. In *King John*, however, Shakespeare's anti-papal rhetoric fires on all cylinders, with astonishing ferocity; and, since there are two entirely different explanations of this play's origins, it is worth pausing, to ask how they reflect on the dramatist's religion.

*King John* used to be thought a revision of *The Troublesome Reign of John King of England,* an anonymous, two-part play first published in 1591. When it was still fashionable to hold that Shakespeare began his writing career as a 'play-patcher' (cf. p. 60), or reviser of other men's work, this explanation of the two puzzlingly similar King John plays was inevitable. In more recent times, however, the play-patcher theory has been pretty well abandoned, the relationship of the two plays has been re-examined, and J. S. Smart and Peter Alexander proposed that *Troublesome Reign,* far from being the 'source' of *King John,* should be seen as a reconstruction of Shakespeare's play. (Copyright did not exist in Queen Elizabeth's time; when a play proved to be popular, another play with more or less the same story was not infrequently written for a rival company, as in the case of *The Taming of the Shrew* and *The Taming of a Shrew.*) The two King John plays present very much the same events and characters, with some differences of emphasis – notably in their anti-Catholic propaganda. In *King John,* the King sends Falconbridge back to England to 'shake the bags / Of hoarding abbots' (III.3.6 ff.), and Falconbridge later reports that he collected large sums from 'the clergymen' (IV.2.141 ff.). Instead of briefly alluding to these exactions, *Troublesome Reign* contains a comic scene with Falconbridge 'leading a Friar, charging him to show where the Abbot's gold lay'; the Friar points out the Abbot's chest, it is broken open and reveals the Abbot's 'treasure' – a beautiful nun.

> *Friar.* O, I am undone! Fair Alice the nun
> Hath took up her rest in the Abbot's chest.
> Sancte benedicite, pardon my simplicity!
> Fie, Alice, confession will not salve this trangression.

The author, with obvious relish, demonstrates that friars and nuns are money-hoarders, fornicators and hypocrites. And towards the end of the play, where *King John* merely reports that the King 'is poisoned by a monk' (V.6.23 ff.), *Troublesome Reign* again inserts additional material – a scene in which the monk discloses the intended murder to his Abbot and is absolved in advance, and another scene that dramatises the poisoning.

Formerly, when it was taken for granted that Shakespeare 'revised' *Troublesome Reign,* it seemed that he toned down its anti-Catholic feeling by omitting these scenes of crude propaganda. Such a view of gentle Shakespeare's good taste will have to be abandoned by those who hold that *King John* preceded *Troublesome Reign*: they can say that the writer of the second play vulgarised it by adding the friar scenes, but they make Shakespeare directly responsible for the anti-Catholic chauvinism, the appeal to the mob, which is the life-blood of *King John*. He devised the plot, inventing the Bastard Falconbridge, giving a central importance to Cardinal Pandulph as universal manipulator, and omitting Magna Carta; that is, he re-wrote history (as he found it in Holinshed) to emphasise the threat from Rome, instead of merely translating another man's dramatised account of John's reign into more effective dialogue. Comparing the king's defiance of Rome in Holinshed and the two plays we can see how Shakespeare does his utmost to arouse anti-papal fury.

   (i) [King John wrote to the Pope in 1207] that he marvelled not a little what the Pope meant, in that he did not consider how necessary the friendship of the King of England was to the see of Rome, sith there came more gains to the Roman church out of that kingdom than out of any other realm on this side the mountains. He added hereto, that for the liberties of his crown he would stand to the death, if the matter so required. ...

                                        (Holinshed, iii, 171)

(ii) *K. John.*  What earthy name to interrogatories
               Can task the free breath of a sacred king?
               Thou canst not, cardinal, devise a name
               So slight, unworthy and ridiculous,
               To charge me to an answer, as the pope.
               Tell him this tale; and from the mouth of England
               Add thus much more, that no Italian priest
               Shall tithe or toll in our dominions;
               But as we, under God, are supreme head,
               So under Him that great supremacy,
               Where we do reign, we will alone uphold
               Without th'assistance of a mortal hand:
               So tell the pope, all reverence set apart
               To him and his usurp'd authority.
  *K. Phi.*  Brother of England, you blaspheme in this.
  *K. John.*  Though you and all the kings of Christendom
               Are led so grossly by this meddling priest,
               Dreading the curse that money may buy out;
               And by the merit of vild gold, dross, dust,
               Purchase corrupted pardon of a man,
               Who in that sale sells pardon from himself;
               Though you and all the rest so grossly led
               This juggling witchcraft with revenue cherish,
               Yet I alone, alone do me oppose
               Against the pope, and count his friends my foes.

(iii) *King John.* And what hast thou or the Pope thy master to do to demand of me how I employ mine own? Know, Sir Priest, as I honour the Church and holy churchmen, so I scorn to be subject to the greatest prelate in the world. Tell thy master so from me, and say John of England said it, that never an Italian priest of them all, shall have either tithe, toll or polling penny out of England, but as I am King so will I reign next under God, supreme head both over spiritual and temporal; and he that contradicts me in this, I'll make him hop headless.[23]

Is it really conceivable that a dramatist brought up as a Catholic, a former servant of Alexander Hoghton and Sir Thomas Hesketh, would wish to write so venomously of Rome? Let us remember that about ten years would have passed since William Shakeshafte worked for Sir Thomas Hesketh (in 1581 or 1582) if *King John* was composed, as I believe, in 1590 or 1591:[24] and that this was a decade when the menace of Rome, as seen by English Protestants, increased alarmingly. Leaving aside the treason trials of seminary priests, there was the Babington conspiracy to murder the Queen (1585-6); the trial and execution of Mary, Queen of Scots, who was accused of encouraging Babington (1586-7); the Spanish Armada, expected for some years before 1588, and, it was rumoured, soon to be followed by a second attempt; and the murder of Henry III, King of France, after he joined forces with the Huguenots against the Catholic League, by a fanatic monk (1589) – this last almost certainly the immediate inspiration for the writing of *King John*. It goes against the grain to think of 'gentle Shakespeare' as a turncoat, inflaming the mob against his former friends, if that is how we interpret his play. Considering, though, that *King John* chiefly attacks the pope's temporal claims, and that loyal English Catholics felt free to defend the Queen against Catholic invaders, we may take a more lenient view: in 1590–1 Shakespeare detested Rome's intrigues and abuses, but nowhere stoops to rabble-rousing against English Catholics, as *Troublesome Reign* does in the friar scenes.

That having been said, it is still surprising – some will say shocking – that a former Catholic would choose to write a play like *King John*. The theory that Shakespeare began life as a Catholic, changed religion, wrote *King John* (perhaps spurred on by Lord Strange, his patron, or merely hoping to please Lord Strange), is disconcerting, I admit; it gives a less flatteringly consistent picture of the dramatist than the traditional one, that he was born a Protestant, wrote some anti-Catholic plays and died a Protestant. But we must never lose sight of the fact that the poet who described himself in the sonnets was a most unusual man. His love-hate relationship with the Dark Lady may even help us to understand how he felt about the Whore of Babylon: not long after *King John* he wrote *Romeo and Juliet* (?1591), where the 'holy friar' represents good sense and moderation; and in *Hamlet* (?1600) he relapsed into a Catholic view of purgatory, in the Ghost's statement that it is doomed 'for a certain term' to fast in fires 'Till the foul crimes done in my days of nature / Are burnt and *purged* away' (I.5.12–13). I find it easier to imagine that a former Catholic might slip into this way of thinking than that a Protestant writer who had never been a Catholic would do so.

There is a similar 'lapsed Catholicism' in *Measure for Measure*. The Duke-as-friar, confessor to Angelo, takes advantage of his disguise to intrigue incessantly, trying to make rings round those who trust him – very much as Catholic priests played games with other men's lives according to Protestant propaganda (compare Marlowe's *Massacre at Paris* or Middleton's *Game at Chess*); and the play's Catholic ramifications, of course, were Shakespeare's additions to the story (Isabella's wish to be a nun; the 'friar', and his officious meddling). Critics of *Measure for Measure* have not paid as much attention as one might expect to its insistent Catholicism, which must have affected the audience-response in 1603–4. Would Protestants at the Globe have sympathised with a novice belonging to the sisterhood of Saint Clare when Angelo tells her to yield up 'thy body to my will', or when the Duke proposes marriage to her? Would she have worn her novice's habit right through the play, even when the Duke proposes? (Modern producers usually get Isabella to change her clothes as quickly as possible: they want a 'feminine' heroine, at all costs.) Would they have sympathised with a friar who takes it upon himself to play the role of 'power divine'? Isabella's willingness to go along with the friar's proposed bed-trick, after she had so roundly condemned the cohabitation of Claudio and Juliet – an inconsistency that has puzzled many commentators – might well be viewed, by a Protestant audience, as another example of Catholic authoritarianism: a novice *must* suppress her conscience when a 'good father' orders her to. The play is not overtly anti-Catholic, yet it activates latent anti-Catholic feeling – while at the same time it manages to present a Catholic point of view persuasively from the inside. This entirely Shakespearian complication of the story, which now centres on a nun and a friar who do *not* arouse the normal Protestant hysteria, is as revealing as the vision of purgatory in *Hamlet*.

Shakespeare's detailed knowledge of Samuel Harsnet's *A Declaration of Egregious Popish Impostures* (1603) has been demonstrated by Kenneth Muir and others. When he wrote *King Lear*, probably in 1605, Shakespeare echoed Harsnet's 284-page treatise in various ways (adopting the unusual names of devils such as Modo and Mahu, Frateretto, Fliberdigibbet, etc., and borrowing other unfamiliar words and phrases, such as 'hysterica passio'.[25]) Why did he read this long-winded exposure of 'popish impostures'? Clearly there was much general interest, witnessed by a stream of books all concerned with the same topic – John Darrell's *A Brief Narration of the Possession of W. Sommers* (1598) and *A Brief Apology proving the Possession of W. Sommers* (1599); Samuel Harsnet's *A Discovery of the fraudulent Practices of J. Darrell* (1599); Darrell's reply, *A Detection of that sinful and ridiculous Discourse of S. Harshnet (sic)* (1600), and *A True Narration of the Vexation by the Devil of 7. Persons in Lancashire* (1600); George More's *A True Discourse concerning the Possession of 7 Persons in one Family in Lancashire* (1600); John Deacon and John Walker, *A Summary Answer to Master Darrell his Books* (1601); *The Reply of J. Darrell* (1602) – and a number of other books that appeared at the same time. As is already evident from two of the titles, some of the 'fraudulent practices' involved Catholics, and their opponents, in Lancashire. Harsnet's *Declaration* of 1603 described the activities of Catholic priests and their supporters in the 1580s, and therefore mentioned names that would particularly interest William Shakespeare if, as I have argued, he worked for some years for Alexander Hoghton, Sir Thomas Hesketh and Lord Strange. For example, Harsnet printed 'the confession of Richard Mainy, gentleman', dated 1602, in which Mainy stated that about fourteen years ago (i.e. in 1588) the Privy Council 'did write their letters unto Ferdinando, then Lord Strange, to examine me' (p. 258 ff): 'it seemeth they had been informed that I should publish how I was possessed with certain wicked spirits, and of them dispossessed by some priests of the Catholic Roman Church, and that I should take upon me, in company where I came, to justify the same. So as being called before the said Lord Strange, he demanded of me whether I had given out such speeches. He examined me upon my oath.' Shakespeare, if one of Lord Strange's Men at this time, would be bound to have heard of the examination of suspected Catholics; and he would also be interested in Harsnet's references to 'Master Salisbury that was executed' (p. 244), one of many to the Babington conspiracy ('Salisbury' was the older brother of Sir John Salusbury of Lleweni: cf. Chapter IX, above); and in Harsnet's account of 'the three worthy champions sent from his Holiness and from hell, for firework[s] here in England, about *anno* 82, Cottam, Brian, and Campian' (pp. 118–19, 216, 249), Cottam being the brother of the former Stratford schoolmaster, John Cottom (cf. p. 40 above). One can see, therefore, that anyone with Lancashire connections who was aware of the Lancashire implications of the Darrell–Harsnet pamphlets would expect

Harsnet's *Declaration* of 1603 to name sensitive names – perhaps even Shakespeare's own.

To continue this very selective survey of Shakespeare's Catholic allusions: in *Macbeth* he dragged in Father Henry Garnet, the Jesuit who was tried for complicity in the Gunpowder Plot: 'Faith, here's an equivocator that could swear in both the scales against either scale; who committed treason enough for God's sake, yet could not equivocate to heaven' (II.3.10 ff.). Towards the end of his life he again echoed an uncompromisingly Protestant attitude in an aside given to Henry VIII, 'I abhor / This dilatory sloth and tricks of Rome' (II.4, a scene generally attributed to Shakespeare). Here, as in *Henry VI* and *King John*, there can be little doubt that the dramatist himself detested the tricks of Rome – after all, we must assume that he chose to write these plays. What is significant, however, is not that he normally wrote as one would expect from a committed Protestant, but that he sometimes reverted to a Catholic viewpoint – which was most unusual in the drama of his day.

The plays, we may therefore say, give some support to the theory that Shakespeare belonged to a Catholic family. It is in the nature of things that the external evidence should be meagre, since Catholics were persecuted and tried to keep their religion a secret; nevertheless, contemporary or near-contemporary witnesses suggest that Shakespeare and his father and his daughter were Catholics. In Shakespeare's own case we may rush to the wrong conclusion simply because he seems to have been a Protestant from the 1580s, during his active writing career, until the year of his death. His will (drawn up in January 1616, and revised in March)[26] is also Protestant in its phrasing. I would not rule out the possibility, however, that a priest was fetched when he lay dying, and that 'he died a papist' – a report that originated with an Anglican clergyman who lived near Stratford, in Gloucestershire and Coventry,[27] and who had no motive for untruthfulness. Former Catholics *have* been known to return to the fold on their death-bed; if it happened in 1616 one can only hope that there was less domestic pressure than in the case of Evelyn Waugh's Lord Marchmain.

# XI

# Conclusion

This book presents a very different picture of the young William Shakespeare from the traditional one. It will be useful to draw attention to some of the differences, and, bringing together the seemingly unrelated conclusions of separate chapters, to ask which are probable and which merely possible.

Aubrey's story that Shakespeare had been in his younger years 'a schoolmaster in the country' has never been seriously challenged, but those who accepted it have doubtless assumed that 'in his younger years' meant in the middle or later 1580s; and such an assumption would be natural at a time when traditionalists held that Shakespeare only started to write plays in 1590–1. The theory, which is steadily gaining ground, that Shakespeare wrote plays for some years before 1590, opens up the possibility that his schoolmastering must be pushed back as well. That he worked as an assistant teacher from the age of sixteen or so is not, in itself, as surprising as the suggestion that he started life as a Catholic and served for a while in the Catholic households of Alexander Hoghton and Sir Thomas Hesketh. Yet this idea, that Shakespeare could have been a Catholic, is not new either – and additional evidence has recently come to light which supports it in other ways. I anticipate that there will be strenuous opposition to Chapter X – though, considering how slowly Queen Elizabeth's government turned the screws and brought pressure to bear on English Catholics, in the 1560s and 1570s, and how many Catholics became Protestants in the 1580s, a Catholic upbringing cannot be thought improbable, especially when one also recalls that three Stratford schoolmasters in the 1570s were closely associated with the Jesuits.[1]

Let us brace ourselves, then, for howls of anguish about a Catholic Shakespeare, and proceed with our assessment. This book restates views that others have also advocated – the schoolmaster in the country, Shakespeare's 'early start' as a dramatist, his Catholicism. I have introduced a new element by focusing on John Cottom, the

# Conclusion

Stratford schoolmaster who could have recommended Shakespeare to Alexander Hoghton in far-off Lancashire. This led to the new suggestion that, if 'Shakeshafte' was Shakespeare, he need not have served Alexander Hoghton as a full-time 'player', but could have taken up playing as a sideline, being initially engaged as a teacher. All this, I hear the reader mutter, is *possible* – but surely it cannot be said to be *proved*! At this point I would like to distinguish between two groups in the 'Lancashire connection', the second of which may seem to have weaker claims than the first. (1) Like E. K. Chambers and others, I consider it probable that Shakespeare worked for a while as one of Lord Strange's Men. My discussions of *The Phoenix and the Turtle* and of the Stanley epitaphs belong to the same group – let us call it the 'Stanley connection'. (2) On the face of it the other group – the 'Hoghton connection' – appears to be possible rather than probable. There are threads that link William Shakespeare and Alexander Hoghton (John Cottom), Hoghton and Hesketh (Fulk Gillam, the musical instruments), Shakespeare and Hesketh (Thomas Savage), Shakespeare and Hoghton again (John Weever); yet some of this intricate criss-crossing of individuals living far apart in Stratford, Lancashire and London could just be explained as a series of coincidences. Thomas Savage could have been a friend of John Heminges rather than of Shakespeare (in 1611 Heminges lived in one of Savage's houses), and Weever could have heard of Shakespeare from his Cambridge acquaintances rather than from the Hoghtons. For this reason I do not think of Savage and Weever as decisively establishing the 'Hoghton connection'; they are, let us say, supportive attachments. The 'Hoghton connection' seems to me a distinct possibility, supported as it is by the local traditions that link Shakespeare with the Hoghtons and with Rufford, by Alexander Hoghton's reference to William Shakeshafte in 1581, and by Beeston's statement that Shakespeare worked in his youth as 'a schoolmaster in the country.' And yet it would have to be relinquished as nothing more than a possibility, were it not for one other crucial factor. The discovery that John Cottom, the Stratford schoolmaster, was also linked with the Hoghton family makes a significant difference and, I think, converts a possibility into a probability.

While I do not claim that all the suggestions in this book are equally probable, I shall now set them out, for the reader's convenience, in chronological order. This will make it easier to relate one to another, and to compare my account of Shakespeare's earlier years with the traditional one. Some non-controversial dates and 'facts' are added, since new suggestions must tie in with what we already know – or think we know – about John and William

Shakespeare. The dates of Shakespeare's plays, I must emphasise, are highly controversial; I have not assigned a date to every play, but where a date is indicated I have given some reasons for it elsewhere.[2]

| | |
|---|---|
| 1564 | William Shakespeare born. |
| 1570 | John Shakespeare accused of large-scale usury and illegal wool-dealing in the Exchequer. |
| 1577 | John Shakespeare stops attending 'halls' at Stratford. |
| 1579 | John Cottom begins to teach in Stratford (July). |
| 1580–1 | William Shakespeare employed as assistant teacher by Alexander Hoghton. |
| 1580 | Thomas Hoghton I dies abroad (June); Thomas Cottam captured and imprisoned in England. |
| 1581 | Alexander Hoghton dies (August); William Shakespeare perhaps works briefly for Thomas II, then for Sir Thomas Hesketh. Richard Hathaway dies (September: he was father of Shakespeare's later wife). Thomas Cottam arraigned (November). John Cottom leaves Stratford (December). |
| 1582 | Shakespeare back in Stratford (by August); William Shakespeare and Anne Hathaway marry (November). |
| 1583 | Susanna Shakespeare born (May). Shakespeare perhaps worked for his father at this time (1582–5?), and became a Protestant. |
| 1585(?)–94 | Shakespeare serves Lord Strange (Earl of Derby, 1593–4). |
| 1586 | John Salusbury marries Ursula Stanley (December), Shakespeare writes *The Phoenix and the Turtle*; also, a 'schoolmaster' play inspired by Ovid and Seneca: *Titus Andronicus*. |
| 1587 | *The Two Gentlemen of Verona*. |
| 1588 | *1 Henry VI*, *The Taming of the Shrew*. |
| 1589 | Robert Greene dedicates *Ciceronis Amor* to Shakespeare's patron, Lord Strange; Thomas Nashe attacks the author of a lost tragedy called *Hamlet*. Shakespeare writes *The Comedy of Errors, 2 Henry VI*. Thomas Hoghton II dies. |
| 1590 | *3 Henry VI, Richard III*; Shakespeare appears in plot of *Seven Deadly Sins*, Part II, as 'Will'. |
| 1591 | Spenser alludes to Shakespeare, 'our pleasant Willy'. Shakespeare writes *King John, Romeo and Juliet*. |
| 1592 | Lord Strange's Men perform Greene's plays (spring); Nashe praises Lord Strange and Shakespeare's |

*1 Henry VI* in *Pierce Penilesse* (summer); Greene's *Groat's Worth of Wit* attacks Shakespeare and implies that he is active as a money-lender (September).[3] Greene dies (September). Shakespeare writes *Love's Labour's Lost* (winter).

1593     Theatres closed because of plague; Shakespeare not included in warrant for Strange's men to travel in country. Shakespeare writes additions (3 pages) for *Sir Thomas More*, and dedicates *Venus and Adonis* to Southampton (S.R. 18 April). Lord Strange succeeds father as 5th Earl of Derby (25 September). Richard Hesketh's conspiracy (tries to persuade 5th Earl to claim crown after Queen Elizabeth).

1594     *Titus Andronicus* published. Ferdinando, Earl of Derby, dies (16 April). *The Rape of Lucrece* dedicated to Southampton (S.R. 9 May). Shakespeare is now a leading member of the Lord Chamberlain's Men.

1595     *A Midsummer Night's Dream* performed at wedding of 6th Earl of Derby (26 January)? Spenser refers to Shakespeare as 'Aetion'.

1596     John Shakespeare applies for a grant of arms, and is said to be 'of good wealth', worth £500.

1597     William Shakespeare buys New Place for £60.

1598     R. Quiney asks William Shakespeare to lend £30. Weever's sonnet 'Ad Gulielmum Shakespeare' written (1597–9?). Francis Meres praises Shakespeare's plays and poems (*Palladis Tamia*, S.R. 7 September).

1599     Richard Hoghton serves as High Sheriff of Lancashire, and is knighted. Weever's *Epigrammes* published. Thomas Savage of Rufford involved in purchase of Globe theatre.

1600–3    Shakespeare writes epitaphs for Sir Thomas and Sir Edward Stanley.

1601     Robert Chester publishes *Love's Martyr*, with Shakespeare's *The Phoenix and the Turtle*. John Shakespeare dies (September).

Claiming that Shakespeare's 'Stanley' and 'Hoghton' connections are not merely possible but probable, I am aware that many questions remain unanswered. Let me attempt to grapple with some that may trouble the wakeful reader. (1) Why should Shakespeare have been sent so far from home when he was only 15 or 16? (Lea in Lancashire is about 130 miles from Stratford as the crow flies). I take it that John Shakespeare wanted his eldest son to join him 'in his own employment' (cf. p. 2), and that William wanted a different career. If a wealthy patron beckoned, the opportunity would seem too good to miss; many boys left home at 15 or earlier, either to serve as pages, or to learn a trade as apprentices, or to go to university. Perhaps, though, Anne Hathaway's interest in her future husband began a year or two before they were married, and John and Mary Shakespeare felt that a wife eight years older than their teenage son would be unsuitable, and therefore sent him away. In the very decade of Shakespeare's marriage the Privy Council intervened in a somewhat similar case, condemning the contrivers of a 'very lewd marriage between Richard Tylden, being a boy about xv years old, and Franklin's niece, being xxv years old', ordering that the young gentleman be sequestered to his guardians during his minority, and that those who persuaded 'the young parties' to marry be punished.[4] If Shakespeare left for Lancashire in 1579 or 1580 he would have been a boy of 15 or 16 and Anne Hathaway would have been 23 or 24: unequal marriages were by no means unheard of at this time, but a considerably older woman was evidently thought a mismatch for a boy 'during his minority'.

(2) Is it likely that Alexander Hoghton would leave an annuity of £2 a year to a youth aged 17 who had only served him one or two years? It would be unusual to reward a young servant so generously, but we should recall that Shakespeare struck those who knew him as an unusually attractive person, and that he received special gifts from other patrons and well-wishers.

> He had the honour [wrote Rowe in 1709] to meet with many great and uncommon marks of favour and friendship from the Earl of Southampton. ... There is one instance so singular in the magnificence of this patron of Shakespeare's that, if I had not been assured that the story was handed down by Sir William Davenant, who was probably very well acquainted with his affairs, I should not have ventured to have inserted that my Lord Southampton at one time gave him a thousand pounds, to enable him to go through with a purchase which he heard he had a mind to.[5]

The sum seems too enormous to be credible, yet we have no reason to doubt that he received 'great and uncommon marks of favour' from Southampton (the dedication of *The Rape of Lucrece* implies 'favour and friendship'); and Heminges and Condell, earlier and better witnesses than Rowe, must have meant something similar when they claimed that the earls of Pembroke and Montgomery 'prosecuted' Shakespeare's plays and their author 'with so much favour'[6] – one assumes that 'favour' again includes financial rewards. All the same, would a master reward a retainer who was little more than a boy? Sir Thomas Hesketh did: 'Also,' he ordained in his will, 'I give to Richard Stannynowght, my foot-boy, xl*s*.' (forty shillings; but this was a single bequest, not an annuity).

(3) If Shakespeare lived for two years with the Hoghtons, and Weever's sonnet suggests that the Hoghton circle remained aware of this former 'servant', why are there no other documents that testify to this long-lasting connection? At the age of 16 or 17 Shakespeare, a minor, is not likely to have been called to witness legal documents, if older men were available: the absence of his name from Hoghton documents prior to Alexander's will is perfectly understandable. And if he was William Shakeshafte he must have changed his religion in the 1580s, whereas the Hoghtons and Heskeths remained Catholics; his earlier employers would therefore see him as a potential informer, which must have cooled their relationship. When Richard Hoghton became a Protestant, after his father's death in 1589, this obstacle would be removed, and perhaps Richard (who was knighted at court in 1599, and no doubt visited London at other times) renewed his acquaintance with Shakespeare. Richard must have been aware of Shakespeare, for presumably he transmitted the family tradition that the dramatist served the Hoghtons in his youth.

(4) Would it not be reasonable to expect John Cottom, the former Stratford schoolmaster, to be a book-lover? Why then did he bequeath no books in his will? One might equally ask why did William Shakespeare bequeath no books in his will? Were there no copies of Holinshed's *Chronicles* or Plutarch's *Lives* at New Place? And why did the meticulous John Weever, a book-lover if ever there was one, likewise pass silently over the books that he surely must have owned? The answer is, quite simply, that books were rarely mentioned in wills at this time; the fact that John Cottom did not refer to books in his will, and that none are listed in the inventory of his goods, is regrettable – but it tells us nothing about his attitude to books or to the greatest writer of his day, and should not be taken as evidence that he owned no books.

(5) If Shakespeare worked for the Hoghtons and Heskeths in Lancashire, is John Cottom the only possible link with Stratford? By no means: it is remarkable that four out of five consecutive Stratford schoolmasters were Lancashire men: Walter Roche (1569–71), Simon Hunt (1571–5), John Cottom (1579–81) and Alexander Aspinall (1582–1624); the only exception was Thomas Jenkins (1575–9), a Londoner. This suggests that there might have been other 'connections' between Stratford and the Hoghtons; it

could be, for instance, that Simon Hunt was a Hoghton tenant, since he went from Stratford to Douay College, where Thomas Hoghton I was an important benefactor. At present, however, we are ignorant of Roche's, Hunt's and Aspinall's territorial roots in Lancashire. Taking Shakespeare's age into account, it seems likely that he left school when either Jenkins or Cottom reigned at the Grammar School: Jenkins was not from Lancashire, whereas Cottom and his family seem to have known the Hoghtons well. Other Stratford–Lancashire contacts may still emerge, but John Cottom remains the obvious link between the two places.

Some questions have, I hope, been disposed of – but by no means all. Much more work needs to be done before we shall discover all we want to know about the schoolmaster in the country. I thought it right to present an interim report since local historians, and others more expert in Elizabethan archives than I am, may be able to pick up the scent where I have lost it. To return once more to John Cottom: if Shakespeare was really recommended to Alexander Hoghton by the Stratford schoolmaster, one would like to see Cottom's books and papers. Every gentleman had his books and papers – might there not be letters from a former pupil, or quartos from a famous dramatist, hidden away in a family collection that no one has thought of prying into for centuries? Cottom's papers would have gone to the only one of his three daughters to survive him, Priscilla; and she, as bad luck would have it, married a man with a common surname, Thomas Walton of Walton le Dale. I was able to trace their descendants to the later seventeenth century and no further. Then, remembering that John Cottom's pedigree was recorded by the Norroy King of Arms in 1613, I wrote to the College of Arms for help. Mr J. P. Brooke-Little (Norroy and Ulster) replied as follows:

> The only recorded pedigree of Walton of Walton le Dale, co. Lancaster, is that entered on 8th April 1665 at the Heralds' Visitation of co. Lancaster made in that year (c37, folio 144r).
>
> The marriage of Thomas Walton to Priscilla Cottam (or Cotham) is entered. Their children were William, John and James. William married Dorothy, daughter of Christopher Anderton of Hurwich, co. Lancaster. Their son Thomas, of Walton le Dale, married Anne, daughter of Roger Hesketh of Turneaker, co. Lancaster, and their sons were William, Thomas and Roger.
>
> There are no other pedigrees of this family, nor could I find any references to printed pedigrees, save that in the Victoria County History of Lancashire mentioned by you.
>
> I also checked all records for later Cottam pedigrees, just in case Priscilla were not an heiress but, as expected, there were none.

Even if one contacted all the Waltons in Preston, or in Lancashire, that would not necessarily lead one to the right family, for John Cottom's papers could have passed again to a female descendant. That such papers once existed cannot be proved; that they still survive, if they ever existed, is doubtful – but the present writer, undeterred, adjures all readers possessed of mouldering family papers to sally forth instantly into lofts, cellars, outhouses etc. and to search for the dusty remains of the Stratford schoolmaster.

It is hard to believe that the Hoghton archives will yield other major surprises, apart from Alexander Hoghton's references to William Shakeshafte. This is because J. H Lumby, preparing *A Calendar of the Deeds and Papers in the Possession of Sir James de Hoghton, Bart.* (1936) over a period of thirty years, has already sifted the material with exemplary care. When Sir Bernard de Hoghton invited me to look through a dozen large strong-boxes crammed with family documents which had not been deposited in the Lancashire Record Office, I was naturally hopeful – yet soon found that Lumby had examined these boxes as well, and had indexed some of their (mostly eighteenth and nineteenth-century) contents. And there are two other reasons for being pessimistic about further Hoghton discoveries.

> Concerning many of the heirlooms of the Hoghtons, including furniture, pictures, plate and other relics of former days, which to-day would have been priceless, a dismal story must be told. The complete disappearance of Sir Charles the fourth baronet's valuable library has already been mentioned. Much else, in the nature of furniture, family portraits, etc., doubtless went the same way during the long years between 1710 and 1870 when the place stood empty and deserted, completely at the mercy of the casual visitor.
> ... But the tale of disaster is not yet complete. About the year 1870 a notable misfortune fell upon the family in the complete destruction of all the pictures, including many family portraits, and much of the family plate, all of which had been stored away for safety in London. These treasures, preparatory to being moved from London to Hoghton, had been placed in a pantechnicon. By some means the conveyance caught fire and its entire contents were destroyed, including a number of valuable papers.[7]

John Weever must have presented a copy of his *Epigrammes* (1599) to Sir Richard Hoghton, the dedicatee, but, like so much else, the volume has disappeared.

John Weever himself is the member of the 'Lancashire connection' most likely to lead us to other discoveries. He was an admirer of Shakespeare, and he had the true magpie habits of a collector, as *Ancient Funeral Monuments* amply illustrates. 'And here let me tell you that amongst many letters of important affairs, which I found in certain chandlers' shops of our parish, allotted to light tobacco pipes and wrap up pennyworths of their commodities, all which I gave to Sir Robert Cotton, Knight and Baronet, the only repairer of ruined antiquity. ...' (pp. 80–1). Weever differed from other antiquarians of his day in being interested in poetry, including very recent poetry, and therefore I believe that his papers, if they are ever located, will be rewarding. My guess is that they may turn up not in the Cottonian Library, which has been known to generations of scholars, but amongst the Vincent manuscripts in the College of Arms. In *Ancient Funeral Monuments* Weever referred several times to 'my dear deceased friend, Augustine Vincent' (To the Reader', and pp. 419, 604, 734), and leaves us in no doubt that Vincent, the Windsor Herald and keeper of the Records in the Tower, shared his interests and greatly helped him. Vincent, in fact, wrote a treatise of roughly the same length as Weever's eighteen introductory chapters on funeral customs, entitled *Parentalia, or Funeral Rites, Ceremonies and Solemnities* (Vincent MS. 87), which shows how closely the two friends worked in tandem; and Vincent, we know, owned a presentation copy of the Shakespeare First Folio, for he recorded that he received it from William Jaggard, the printer, 'anno 1623'. Vincent, in short, appears to have been a Shakespeare enthusiast, like his friend John Weever, and he was definitely a collector. The cataloguing of the many Vincent Manuscripts in the College of Arms goes along steadily, though the end is not yet in sight. There are papers in unidentified hands, and it is probable that in the course of cataloguing unexpected treasures will come to light. Weever's notes on the contemporary poets he knew personally and quoted so freely? or some scraps of Shakespeare? Only time will tell.

# Appendix A. Extracts from wills

(In these extracts I have modernised the spelling and expanded contractions. The punctuation in the wills is minimal, and sometimes confusing; I have changed it here and there, without attempting to modernise it completely.)

1. Alexander Hoghton of Lea, Esq. (3 August 1581; proved 12 September 1581). Extracts printed by G. J. Piccope in *Lancashire and Cheshire Wills* (Second Portion, *CS*, vol. li, 1860). Facsimile of 'Shakeshafte' passage in Oliver Baker, *In Shakespeare's Warwickshire* (1937), p. 298.

In the name of God Amen. The third day of August ... after the Incarnation of Jesus Christ one thousand five hundred eighty-one. I Alexander Hoghton of the Lea in the county of Lancaster, Esquire, being sick in body yet of good & perfect ‹...› memory, thanks be to almighty God, and considering with myself that nothing is more certain than death, nor nothing more incertain & doubtful than the hour of death, and also what great troubles & inconveniences do for the most part grow after the death of those that are possessed of lands or goods for lack of good ordering & disposing of the same in their life-time; therefore & to th'intent no cause of contention or trouble should arise after my decease among my kinsfolks & friends for or concerning any of my possessions goods or chattels; and to th'intent also that my wife & children, if it shall please almighty God to bless me with any, might not be left desolate or unprovided; and that my true and diligent servants which hath taken pains with me in my life-time might be recompensed, the poor people according to my ability relieved, & other deeds of charity performed, and my debts truly paid & discharged. I have already, by sufficient conveyance in the law executed in my life-time, disposed all my manors, messuages, lands & tenements to such uses, intents & purposes as I doubt not but do stand with the pleasure of almighty God, the comfort of all my friends, & the contentation of all good men, and are as I trust to the upholding & maintenance of that house, whereof myself and all my ancestors have lineally descended. And now for the ordering & disposing of my goods & chattels, concerning the which I have heretofore done nothing, and for the making perfect in some points of such conveyances as is aforesaid & for the cases aforesaid, I do make my last will & testament in manner & form following. First I do bequeath my soul into the hands of almighty God, desiring most instantly in my daily prayers that the same may be dissolved from this mortal & w[r]etched body & be with Him in the communion of saints & fellowship of all the company of heaven, when and as soon as it shall please his divine majesty, not doubting but to be saved by the merits & passion of Jesus Christ my only saviour & redeemer, in whom only I do repose my trust & confidence. And my body to be buried in the parish church of Preston, so near that place where my father Sir Richard Hoghton Knight & Dorothy my wife do lie buried as convenient may be. The which I would have done if so be that it shall fortune that God do call me from this transitory life within forty miles of the same church. And I do constitute ordain & make my sole executrix of this my last will & testament Elizabeth my well beloved wife; and if she do refuse to take upon her the charge & administration of the same or shall fortune to die in my life-time, then I will that my loving brother-in-law Thomas Hesketh of Gray's Inn in the county of Middlesex, gentleman, and my trusty & well-beloved servants George Beseley & James Helme shall be my executors, desiring my said wife if she take upon her the same charge & administration, & if she do not then the same Thomas Hesketh, George Beseley & James Helme, that they & ‹...› of them, as they will answer before the tribunal seat of Jesus Christ at the dreadful day of judgement, to execute this my last will in every part & parcel thereof according to the purport & effect thereof, all advantages shifts & escapes which may be found out by curious searching heads out of the common law of England or any other law to the contrary notwithstanding. Item, I will that all my debts shall be paid & discharged at such days & times as they shall be due & payable, as well those & such ... debts as are due & owing by matter in writing, as also all my simple contracts & bargains without writing which can be so sufficient proved to be due, as shall be thought meet & convenient by the supervisors of this my last will & testament or any ‹...› of them. Item, I give & bequeath to Elizabeth my wife all my plate, that is to say as well all my bowls, tuns, spoons & salts as also all her apparel, rings & jewels whatsoever which she hath been accustomed to wear and have during my life-time. Item, it is my will that if the residue of my goods & chattels, my debts & funerals being discharged, and the said several sums of money bestowed in such sort as is aforesaid, do amount unto the sum of two hundred marks, then I give & bequeath to Margaret my bastard daughter, wife to Roger Crichelawe of Charnock Richard in the said county & to all her children the sum of one hundred marks equally to be divided amongst them. And if the residue of my goods & chattels ... do not extend to the sum of two hundred marks, then I give & bequeath to the said Margaret my bastard daughter & to all her children the third part of all my goods & chattels, whatsoever value or sum the same shall then be, extend, amount or come unto, in three parts to be divided, the said third part to be equally divided amongst the said Margaret & her children. The said sum or sums as shall happen to be as aforesaid to be delivered unto the said Roger her husband within six months after my decease. So that he do enter into such sufficient bond as shall be thought convenient by my said supervisors or any two of them for the leaving of the same with the increase thereof after his decease unto the said Margaret & her children or to the survivor or survivors of them. Item, I give & bequeath unto the wife of John Tomlinson th'elder the sum of forty shillings. Item, it is my mind & will that the said Thomas Hoghton of 'brynescoules' my brother shall have all my instruments belonging to musics, & all manner of play clothes if he be minded to keep & do keep players. And if he will not keep & maintain players, then it is my mind & will that Sir Thomas Hesketh knight shall have the same instruments & play clothes. And I most heartily require the said Sir Thomas to be friendly unto Fulk Gillom & William Shakeshafte now dwelling with me & either to take them unto his service or else to help them to some good master, as my trust is he will. Item, I give and bequeath to William Wall, clerk, five pounds. Item, I give and bequeath to Thomas Gryffyne, servant to the said Sir William Wall, twenty shillings. Item, I give unto every one of my servants that shall fortune to be in my service at the time of my decease & is or shall be hired with me for yearly wages, be they men or woman, to every one of them one whole year's wages. And whereas I the said Alexander & the said Thomas Hoghton my younger brother, in consideration of an agreement between the said Thomas & me for the establishing of all my manors lands & tenements after divers remainders upon the said Thomas & the heirs male of his body lawfully begotten, by our deed bearing date the twentieth day of July in the year of our lord God one thousand five hundred & four score ... have granted unto Thomas Fleetwood, son & heir apparent of John Fleetwood of Penwortham in the said county of Lancaster, Esquire, & unto Robert Talbot bastard son of the said John Talbot the annual rent of sixteen pounds thirteen shillings four pence issuing and going out of certain my lands & tenements in Withnell, in the said county of Lancaster, to have ... the said yearly rent to the said Thomas & Robert & their heirs from the day of the decease of me the said Alexander for & during the term of the natural lives & of such person & persons & of the longest liver of them, as I the said Alexander shall declare & appoint in & by my last will & testament in writing, yearly payable at the feast of Pentecost & St Martin the bishop in winter by even portions. And further as by the said deed more at large it doth & may appear, and for so much as the said rent was granted in such sort as is aforesaid unto the said Thomas & Robert only upon trust & confidence reposed by me in them that they & their heirs should suffer such persons as should be nominated & appointed by me to have & enjoy the same in such order & manner as should be by me directed, and not intended nor meant that any profit or commodity should grow thereby unto the said Thomas & Robert or their heirs. The which my intention & meaning I trust that whosoever shall fortune to be the judge for matters in the Chancery from time to time will see duly executed according to equity & good conscience. Therefore for the plain declaration how & in what sort the said rent shall be disposed & how long the same shall continue, it is my will, first, that the said rent shall have continuance unto the said Thomas & Robert & their heirs for & during the natural life & lives & of the longest liver of these my servants, that is to wit, Thomas Barton, William Rigby, Roger Livesey, John Hoghton, Henry Bounde, William Clough, Thomas Coston, John Kitchen, James Pemberton, Robert Tomlinson, Richard Fishwick, John Cotham, Thomas Barker, Henry Browne, Miles Turner, Richard Snape, James Greaves, Thomas Sharp, George Bannister, John Beseley, Thomas Ward, Robert Bolton, John Snape, Roger Dickinson, Fulk Gillom, William Shakeshafte, Thomas Gyllom, William Ascroft, Roger Dugdale & Margery Gerrard. And it is my will that the said rent shall be divided amongst my said servants in manner & form following, so that there shall be yearly due & payable, unto the said Thomas Sharp the sum of three pounds six shillings eight pence, unto the said Thomas Coston twenty shillings, unto the said Thomas Barker twenty shillings, unto the said Roger Dickinson thirteen shillings four pence, unto the said William Ormesheye alias Ascroft thirteen shillings four pence, unto the said Robert Bolton twenty shillings, unto the said Thomas Ward twenty shillings, unto the said Fulk Gyllom forty shillings, unto the said William Shakeshafte forty shillings, unto the said Thomas Gyllom forty shillings & unto the said Roger Dugdale forty shillings. To every of them according to several portions, to have & perceive unto every one of them the said several sums for & during their natural lives. And if it fortune any of them to die living ['Lyvinge', ?leaving] the rest, then it is my will that the portion of that party that shall so die shall be equally divided amongst them that shall survive & so from one to one as long as any of them shall be living, so that the survivor of them all shall have for and during his natural life the said whole and entire rent of sixteen pounds thirteen shillings four pence. And it is my especial desire & I straitly charge the said Thomas Fleetwood & Robert Talbot & their heirs as they will answer me before God that they see my will in this point duly & truly executed. And lastly I give unto my said wife all the residue of my goods & chattels being not before by me bequeathed or given. And I shall most earnestly desire my trusty and loving friends John Talbot of Salebury, Edward Standish of Standish, Esquire, Thomas Fleetwood son & heir apparent of the said John Fleetwood & my brother-in-law Bartholomew Hesketh to be supervisors of this my last will & testament. Witness hereof I have put my hand & seal the day & year first above written, these being witness Thomas Fleetwood, Bartholomew

Hesketh, Robert Park, Adam Boulton, William Wall, clerk, John Houghton & Peter Melling. Debts owing unto me Imprimis Richard Bannister gent of Darwin Hall alias Bannister in Walton xvl. for which he hath pledged to me all his wheat now growing more of the said Richard in lent money xls.

Provided alway and further it is the will & pleasure & the true intent & meaning of me the ‹. . . .› named Alexander Hoghton that all such obligation & bonds wherein any my tenants of Ashton under Lyne are indebted and stand bound unto me the said Alexander my executors or assigns shall be void & no advantage taken thereof either of principal debt or forfeiture by any my executrix or executors, but that my said executrix or executors shall the same release & make void unto my said tenants so bounden, and shall not take any advantage of benefit thereby any ways but the said tenants shall be clearly acquitted exonerated and discharged in every respect by & unto my said executrix or executors to & for the same, for & in consideration & so that the said tenants that so my will is shall be acquitted of their bonds shall not hereafter claim ask or demand of my said executrix or executors or their assigns any debt or duty owing or due by me the said Alexander unto any of the said tenants so acquitted by any means, except such money as Edmund Duckenfylde my servant did last borrow of the said tenants to & for my use. The which it is my will to be discharged as parcel of my debts, desiring the said tenants that they will deal friendly with my said executrix or executors in giving reasonable days for payment of the said money excepted. In witness whereof I the said Alexander have put to my seal to this schedule & the same annexed to my said last will & testament as parcel thereof with my seal in presence of Thomas Fleetwood, Thomas Whittingham, Thomas Barton, Richard Whittingham & Robert Parke.

Memorandum that the said Alexander Hoghton after the writing of his will did, lying upon his death-bed, videlicet, within two days before his death being of good and perfect memory, revocate & call back by express words a certain legacy which before in his written will he had given & bequeathed to one Margaret bastard daughter of the said Alexander wife unto Roger Crichelowe of Charnock Richard and to all her children, & did will & command that the said legacy should be stricken out of the said will and this did he divers times or at the least once in the presence of sundry witness.

Item, he did also lying upon his death-bed that is to say whilst he lay sick after [?alter] a certain schedule made & annexed to his will concerning the making void of certain obligations & bonds wherein his tenants of Ashton under Lyne were bound, being informed that his debts being paid & funerals discharged & the said obligations & all such money as he had appointed to be given again unto his tenants were discharged, that then his wife would have no part of his goods left unto her for her maintenance. He then perceiving the same likely to be true, did will appoint & declare that his intention & meaning was that if so be that his wife should have sufficient furniture for her house meet for her calling, her plate & jewels, which were bequeathed by him unto her and twelve oxen twenty kine & a bull & horses convenient for her & also necessary stuff of husbandry or to the like effect & purpose, that then his will & schedule annexed to the said will concerning the same should therein be performed or else every of them to be answered penny pound like of the residue of his goods and not otherwise.

The last three paragraphs were written out separately and attached to the will. Piccope printed the first of the three ('Provided alway . . . Robert Parke') last. It should be noted that Piccope omitted many words and longer passages without warning the reader.

# Appendix A

Many of those named in Alexander Hoghton's will appear in other contemporary records. I subjoin a list, in alphabetical order, with basic information about Hoghton's friends and servants; more information is of course available. Lumby's *Calendar* is cited below as *Cal.*, and the numbers after *Cal.* refer to document numbers. A.H. is Alexander Hoghton.

Bannister, Richard (gent.). See Livesey, Roger, and *Cal.* 50.

Barton, Thomas (gent.). A.H.'s steward (see p. 17); *Cal.* 50.

Beseley, George (gent.). Bracketed frequently with James Helme in Hoghton documents; both were trusted Hoghton 'servants'. Mentioned 1560 (*Cal.*, 738), etc. An indenture of 1580 names Beseley as 'of Goosnargh gent' (*Cal.* 1403). A George and Ellen Beesley of Goosnargh were the parents of the priests George and Richard Beesley (Godfrey Anstruther, *The Seminary Priests*, 1969).

Bound, Henry. Cf. p. 17, above. A witness, with Thomas I, in 1566 (*Cal.*, 418).

Clough, William. Witness for Thomas I, 1567 (*Cal.*, 353).

Coston, Thomas. Cf. p. 17, above and *Cal.*, 654 (Sir Richard Hoghton is 'to hold Thos. Cosson' to fulfil a covenant, 1615); 671.

Cotham, John. See Chapter IV, 'John Cottom of Tarnacre'. Described as 'gentleman' in his will.

Crichelawe, Roger and Margaret. Perhaps A.H.'s daughter was the Margaret 'Critchlowe', widow, defendant (with William Duddell, James Helme, etc.) *v.* Thomas Hoghton, Esq., in 1584 (*Cal.*, 211). But a Roger 'Crechley' served as cook in 1592 (*The House and Farm Accounts of the Shuttleworths*, ed. J. Harland, CS, 1856, Part I, pp. 75, 79). Thomas, bastard son of Margery 'Croichlawe', appears in Blackburn in 1602 (Tait, *Quarter Sessions*, p. 148).

Fishwick, Richard. Married to Margaret, daughter of Richard Snape (*q.v.*) of Goosnargh (BL, Add. MS. 32,115 [S140]).

Fleetwood, John (Esq.). High Sheriff of Lancashire, 1578. See Hasler. There are copies of his will (1590) in the LRO (damaged), and in PCC (6 Sainberbe).

Fleetwood, Thomas (gent.) Son of above; married Mary, daughter of Sir Richard Sherburne of Stonyhurst. See *Cal.*, 1212, for the grant by A.H. and Thomas II to Thomas Fleetwood and Robert Talbot, 20 July, 1580 (i.e. for the annuities mentioned in A.H.'s will) and below, p. 141.

Gillam, Fulk. See Chapter III (p. 31).

Gillam, Thomas. See p. 32.

Helme, James (cf. Beseley, George). Appears as Hoghton witness in 1561 (*Cal.*, 206), etc. Described as 'of Chipping yeoman' in 1580 (*Cal.*, 1403.) Janet Helme of Chipping, widow, named her son James as one of her two executors (1599), and a James Helme of Chipping, husbandman, made his will in 1633 (BL, Add. MS. 32, 115, fos. 276b, 295b). James Helme, constable of Chipping, was committed in 1605 for allowing an arrested man to escape, and a 'James Helme of Lea' was licensed to buy corn in 1601 (Tait, *Quarter Sessions*, pp. 242, 73). There were several James Helmes in the Preston area (cf. also p. 48).

Hesketh, Bartholomew (Esq.). A.H.'s brother-in-law. Deponent in DL4 29 (39): he was about 42 in 1587, i.e. was born *c.* 1545. Included in a list of Lancashire gentlemen 'not seeming to be recusants but discovered to be dangerous persons' in 1592. Accused of keeping a Catholic schoolmaster (cf. p. 20); examined by Privy Council, 1581, suspected of being Campion's friend, and 1593 (on bond of £500) in connection with Hesketh conspiracy (cf. above, p. 37, and APC, XIII, 256–7; HMC, Hatfield House, IV, 241, 402).

Hesketh, Sir Thomas. See Chapter III: 'Sir Thomas Hesketh of Rufford'.

Hesketh, Thomas (of Gray's Inn, gent.). A.H.'s brother-in-law. Bencher and

Reader of Gray's Inn, 1588; Recorder of Lancaster; M.P., 1597; Attorney of the Court of Wards; knighted 1603 (see *The Stanley Papers*, Part 2, p. 205). Sir Thomas Heneague wrote to Cecil in 1595 that no one in Lancashire has done more to further 'her Majesty's service' against recusants than Mr Hesketh (HMC, Hatfield House, V, 359–60); if, as seems likely, he meant A.H.'s brother-in-law, Thomas may have been the kinsman who denounced Sir Thomas Hesketh's laxness against recusants (cf. p. 35). See Hasler.

Hoghton, Elizabeth. A.H.'s second wife and widow (*Cal.*, 1406). Daughter of Gabriel Hesketh of Aughton, to whom an unknown poet dedicated his poetry (Harleian MS. 7578, no. 5). Shortly after A.H.'s death she married George Warburton, gent., and sued her brothers, Bartholomew and Thomas Hesketh, for properties left to them by A.H. in trust for her. Dead by June, 1599 (cf. above, pp. 12, 28).

Hoghton, Thomas (Esq.). Thomas II, A.H.'s brother: cf. p. 146.

Livesey, Roger. A.H.'s 'bailiff of Hoghton, Wheelton and other places'; died not long after A.H. His widow, Mary Livesey, took Thomas II to law, and many Hoghton friends and retainers deposed or were named as witnesses, including Richard Bannister, Thomas Barton, Bartholomew Hesketh, Richard Hoghton of Park Hall, Richard Whittingham, and Robert Swansey of Brindle, gent., A.H.'s attorney (DL4 29 (39)).

Melling, Peter. A Hoghton tenant in Lea (*Cal.*, 206); made his will in 1583 (BL, Add. MSS. 32,106 fo. 317b; 32,115 (M 18)).

Pemberton, James. Catholic recusants brought before the ecclesiastical commissioners in 1584 included James Pemberton of Whiston the younger and the wife of James Pemberton the elder (*CRS*, V, 69 ff.). James Pemberton witnessed Sir Richard Hoghton's 'settlement' of 1607 (DDCl 916).

Snape, Richard. Richard Snape of Goosnargh made his will in 1627 (Add. MS. 32,115 (S140)). See Fishwick, Richard.

Standish, Edward (Esq.). One of A.H.'s supervisors. J.P.; died 1603. Married Ellen, daughter of Sir William Radcliffe of Ordsall (Gillow, *Map*, p. 30); when A.H. married his first wife, Dorothy Ashton, her stepfather was Sir W. Radcliffe of Ordsall (*Cal.* 1396).

Talbot, John (Esq.). There are extracts from his will, dated 23 Jan., 24 Eliz., in the Bodleian (MS. Top. Lancs. C6, fo. 2b): he leaves all goods and chattels, real and personal, 'unto Robert Talbot my base begotten son'. Addressed as 'the Right Worshipful Mr John Talbot Esq.' by the priest John Amias, 8 June 1580, and clearly a Catholic (*CRS*, V, 319).

Talbot, Robert. Natural son of above. Married Elizabeth, natural daughter of Sir Richard de Hoghton, a half-sister of A.H. (Miller, *Hoghton Tower*, p. 149). See Fleetwood, Thomas.

Wall, William. Thomas Wall, clerk, vicar of Preston, named William Wall as his second son in 1599 (Add. MS. 32,115 (W26)).

Ward, Thomas. Helped to defend Thomas Hoghton at Lea in 1589. See also *Cal.*, 356.

Whittingham, Richard (gent.). A deponent in DL4 29 (39): see Livesey, Roger. Bracketed with George Beseley in 1560 (*Cal.*, 738).

Whittingham, Thomas (gent.). See *Cal.*, 909.

N.B. Most of A.H.'s closer friends are shown to have been known or suspected Catholics in *Lord Burghley's Map of Lancashire in 1590*, ed. Joseph Gillow (1907). See Fleetwood, John and Thomas; Hesketh, Gabriel;

Hesketh, Sir Thomas; Hoghton family; Standish, Edward; Talbot family, etc. Miller (*Hoghton Tower*, p. 156) mentions that in 1575 the Bishop of Chester wrote to the Privy Council about recusancy in his diocese, and named Alexander Hoghton as one of those 'of longest obstinacy against religion'.

As already stated (p. 24), Alexander Hoghton's will refers back to a deed or grant of 20 July 1580, in which he made preliminary arrangements for the annuities to be paid to his 'servants'. This deed is printed from DDHo GG1090 (Lumby, *Calendar*, no. 1212).

To all Christian people to whom this present writing shall come ... Alexander Hoghton of the Lea in the county of Lancaster, Esquire, & Thomas Hoghton the younger brother of the said Alexander, send greeting in our lord God everlasting. Know you that we the said Alexander Hoghton & Thomas Hoghton for divers good & reasonable causes & considerations ... have given granted & confirmed, & by these presents for us & our heirs do give grant & confirm unto Thomas Fleetwood, gentleman, son & heir apparent of John Fleetwood of Penwortham in the said county, Esquire, & Robert Talbot, gentleman, bastard son of John Talbot of Salesbury in the said county, Esquire, one yearly rent of sixteen pounds thirteen shillings & four pence of good & lawful money of England, to be issuing & going out of all & every those messuages, cottages, lands, tenements and hereditaments with th'appurtenances mentioned & expressed hereafter in these presents, ŝituate lying & being in Withnell in the said county of Lancaster & in the several tenures of those whose names hereafter severally be named & mentioned, that is to wit one messuage or tenement now or late in the holding or occupation of John Benson, of the yearly rent of xvjs vijd ... [To save space I cite the remaining tenures as a list of names and rents.] The late wife of Edmond Woodd [i.e. the wife of the late E. Wood], 25s 8d; Richard Gar‹sting›, 14s; Thomas Watson, 12s 10d; James Haydocke, 25s 8d; Thomas Catterall, 17s 1d; John Haworthe, 16s 11d; the late wife of George B‹. .›ye, 21s 5d; Richard Livesey, 8s 8d; Christopher Marsden, 14s; Christopher Wilkinson, 16s 6d; Adam Blacklatch, 2s 4d; Thomas Clayton, 11s 9d; John Lucas, 8s 6d; Geoffrey Marley, 12s; John Hoghton de land, 6s 6d; Oliver Lucas 6s 4d; John Abbot, 16s 4d; Thomas Osboldston, 7s; Thomas Bolton, 23s 11d; the late wife of Richard Woodcock, 22s 2d; Nicholas Darwin, 15s 1d; the late wife of John Aspeden, 2s 4d; Alexander Hoghton, 3s; the tenants of 'bremecroffte' [cf. Lumby, index: *Brimmicroft*], 6s 8d. To have perceive levy & take the said yearly rent of sixteen pounds thirteen shillings four pence unto the said Thomas Fleetwood & Robert Talbot & their heirs from the day of the decease of me the said Alexander Hoghton for & during the term of the natural life of such person & persons & of the longest liver of them as I the said Alexander Hoghton shall declare & appoint in or by my last will & testament in writing, yearly payable & to be paid at the feast of Pentecost & St Martin the bishop in winter by even portions, & the first payment thereof to commence & begin at the first feast of the said feasts that shall next ensue & follow after the death of me the said Alexander Hoghton. And if it fortune that the said yearly rent of sixteen pounds thirteen shillings four pence to be behind & unpaid in part or in all at any of the said feasts in which it ought to be paid, being lawfully demanded, that then & so often it shall & may be lawful unto the said Thomas Fleetwood & Robert Talbot & their heirs during the term & time aforesaid, into the said messuages lands tenements & other the premises to enter & distrain, and the distress & distressor then & there ‹. . .› take away, impound & with them to detain & keep until such time as they shall be of the said yearly rent of sixteen pounds thirteen shillings four pence together with the arrearages thereof, if any such ‹be›, well & truly contented satisfied & paid. Provided always that if I the said Alexander Hoghton do not declare & appoint in & by my last will & testament in writing some person or persons during whose life or lives the said yearly rent ... may have continuance according to the grant aforesaid, that then this present grant & every matter & thing therein contained shall be merely frustrate void & of none effect force or strength in the law [*interlined*: any‹thing afore› said to the contrary notwithstanding]. In witness whereof we the said Alexander Hoghton & Thomas Hoghton to this our present writing have set our seals. Given the xxth day of July in the two & twentieth year of the reign of our sovereign lady Elizabeth, by the grace of God Queen of England, France & Ireland, defender of the faith, &c. [*Signed:*] Alexander Hoghton, Thomas Hoghton. [Sealed and delivered in the presence of eight witnesses, whose signatures are partly illegible. They include: ‹...› Fleetwood, Thomas Southworth, Thomas Morte, John Talbot, Alexander Rigby, William Hulton.]

2. Sir Thomas Hesketh of Rufford (20 June 1588). Extracts printed in (*a*) *The Stanley Papers*, Part 2, p. 124 ff.; (*b*) W. G. Procter, 'The Manor of Rufford and the Ancient Family of the Heskeths' (*HSLC*, 1908, LIX, 104 ff.); manuscript copies are found in (*c*) Add. MS. 32,104 (inaccurate: cf. above, p. 35), and (*d*), the Cheshire Record Office (EDA 2/2, fo. 142b). The following extracts are taken chiefly from (*a*) and (*d*).

'I resign my soul into the hands and to the mercy of the most mighty and everlasting God my only maker and redeemer and sanctifier, trusting by the death and passion of our Lord Jesus Christ and by the shedding of his most precious blood I shall rest with him for ever as one of his elect, and my body I will shall be buried by God his grace and sufferance in the new work and chancel of the chapel of Rufforth in such place, manner and sort as I shall hereafter appoint.' (See p. 36, above). He bequeathes property in Mawdesley and Croston to 'Thomas Hesketh my second son'; to Richard Hesketh, 'my third son ... my capital messuage called Beconsall'; other bequests to 'Thomas Hesketh my bastard son' and 'Hugh Hesketh my bastard son', to 'Henry Squire and Dorothy his wife, my daughter', to 'Richard Hesketh and Christopher Hesketh my bastard brethren'.

Annuities to 'servants' include one to 'Hugh Haughton my servant': 'during all his natural life one annuity or annual rent charge' of £20; one to Diggory Rishton (£6 13s 4d p.a.); one to John Spencer (5 marks, i.e. £1 13s 4d p.a.). 'Item I give to Tristram Knowles, Thomas Backhouse, Thomas Farbeck, Richard Baker, Nicholas Conse, Thomas Werden, Henry Squire, James Tomson, Richard Davie, every one of them xls. [forty shillings] yearly during their natural lives. ... Also I give to Richard Stannynowght my foot-boy xls.'

'To Dame Alice Hesketh, my wife, the third part of all my goods.' To Robert Hesketh, his son and heir, Sir Thomas bequeathes his chain of gold, two silver cans, his best silver basin and ewer, the newest hangings, the cup and cover whereon was engraved the spread eagle, all beds, bed coverings, carpets, cushions whereupon his arms or crest were either carved or wrought with needle, and all armour, munitions and weapons wherewith to serve her Majesty.

As executors he named Sir Richard Sherburne, Henry Stanley of the Cross, Esq., Thomas Hesketh of Gray's Inn, gent., and Hugh Hesketh, his bastard son. The supervisors to be John Towneley, Esq., and Robert Hesketh, his son and heir.

3. Thomas Savage of Rufford and London (3 October 1611). PCC (78 Wood), contemporary copy.

'In the name of God the Father, God the Son and God the Holy Ghost, in whose name I was baptised and in whom only I believe to be saved. Amen. I, Thomas Savage, citizen and goldsmith of London, being sick in body but of perfect mind and memory.... First I bequeath my soul into thy hands O God – Father, Son and Holy Ghost. Thou hast first made me, and Thou hast given thy Son to become man, who died for my sins and for the sins of the people. O Father, for this thy Son's sake, have mercy upon me. O Lord Jesus Christ, thou Son of God which hast bought me with thy precious blood by one oblation sufficient for all, I believe in Thee. ...'

Savage's goods to be divided into three parts: one third for his wife Alice; one third for his children (excluding Richard, his eldest son, already provided for); one third for the executor, to pay for legacies etc. to be specified.

To Richard, eldest son, the house in Silver St, parish of St. Olave's, which 'Mr William Peirson, goldsmith, now inhabiteth'.

To Alice, his wife, the house he now dwells in, in Great Wood St, in the parish of St. Alban.

To John Savage, youngest son, the house in Addle St, parish of St Mary in Aldermanbury, 'wherein Mr John Heminges, grocer, now dwelleth'. (This is John Heminges the actor, a member of Shakespeare's company, who belonged to the Grocers' Company.) It should be noted that Richard Savage also had two sons to whom he did not leave houses: Thomas and George.

To Elizabeth Savage, daughter, the house in Addle St in which Mr John Wotton, gent., now dwelleth.

Thomas Chappell, John Rowden, Wm. Adderley and Wm. Tribecke, on 30 May last, sold to Thomas Savage a 'messuage or tenement called The George, with all shops, cellars ... gardens', in St Sepulchre's, London, occupied by Arthur Strangwayes, together with four shops. These are bequeathed 'unto the parson and churchwardens of the parish church of St Alban in Great Wood St in London and to their successors'. To the poor people of the above parish, forty shillings.

'Item, I give and bequeath unto the poor people of the town of Rufforth in the parish of Croston in the County of Lancaster, where I was born, the sum of forty shillings to be distributed amongst them at the discretion of my brother-in-law John Palmer, Thomas Spencer, Thomas Awly and Hugh Watkinson or so many of them as shall be then living at the time of my decease.'

To 'the worshipful Company of Goldsmiths in London, whereof I myself am a free member, one spout pot of silver white to weigh thirty ounces', and £8 'to make them a supper'.

To 'my mother Janet Savage the sum of ten pounds, to be paid within two months next after my decease if she be then living'.

'Item, I give unto my two sisters Cicely Peacock and Katherine Palmer to each of them the sum of five pounds, to be paid to them within six months next after my decease ... Item, I give unto my brothers-in-law John Palmer and Ambrose Peacock to each of them twenty shillings to make each of them a ring of gold, if their wives be then living.' To Thomas Peacock, son of sister Cicely, £3; to each of his brothers and sisters, twenty shillings.

'Unto my cousin Francis Savage of Rufforth the sum of forty shillings. ... And to each of his children twenty shillings.'

'Unto my cousin Hesketh, widow, late wife of Thomas Hesketh of Rufforth, the sum of twenty shillings.'

'Unto my mother-in-law Mrs Wootton, widow, three pounds to make her a ring of gold. ... Unto my sister Sara Flint three pounds.'

'Item, I give unto my fellows the sea-coal m‹..›ters of the city of London', £3 for a dinner.

'Unto my cousin Anne Leland the sum of three pounds and a mourning gown.' Savage appoints 'my trusty friend Robert Hill, citizen and merchant tailor of London, the full and sole executor', and gives him £10. He appoints 'my very loving friends Mr Doctor Lister and Mr John Jackson to be my overseers', and gives each of them £3.

4. John Cottom of Tarnacre (17 July 1616). Lancashire Record Office.

In the name of God Amen. I, John Cottom of Tarnacre in the parish of St Michael upon Wyre in the county of Lancaster, gentleman, being now of good and perfect remembrance, do ordain and make this my last will and testament in manner and form following. First, I give and bequeath my soul unto almighty God my maker and redeemer, by whose death and passion I trust to be saved and my body to be buried at the discretion of my executors. Item, I give and bequeath all my lands, leases, goods and chattels to my daughter Priscilla and her assigns during her natural life, my debts funeral charges and legacies discharged. Item, I give unto William Walton, son to Thomas Walton and Priscilla, and to his heirs for ever, all my lands, leases lying within Tarnacre and Sowerby within the aforesaid parish of St Michael, yielding and paying out of the same to John Walton his brother one hundred pounds, to James Walton his other brother one hundred pounds, and to Ann Walton his sister £200, to be paid in 4 years after his entrance unto the whole. And for default of payment of the aforesaid sums yearly for four years after to the aforesaid John, James and Anne to charge my lands therewithal for those years. Item, I ordain and make Thomas Walton my son-in-law my sole and lawful executor of this my last will and testament, in witness whereof I have hereunto set my hand and seal the day and year above

written in the presence of                     John Cottom
per me Thomas Walmesley
curate de Walton in le Dale
[the marks of two witnesses]

Attached, two statements, one by Thomas Walmesley, curate of Walton le Dale: on or about 17 July he was sent for to the decedent to be a witness unto his will; he found the will ready drawn, and then the decedent signed, sealed and delivered the writing to Mr Thomas Walton, sole executor; Cottom asked Walmesley to read the will aloud, which he did three several times; Cottom then took the will into his own hands, lying in his bed, and perused the same, and acknowledged it. The second statement confirms.

# Appendix A

Inventory of John Cottom's goods at Tarnacre, made by George Brown and others, 27 July 1616.

Imprimis, 4 pair of breeches 50s; 4 doublets 30s; 4 jerkins 25s; 4 cloaks £3 6s 8d; 3 pair of stockings 10s; 2 hats 10s; 3 pair of shoes, 2 pair of boots, one pair of spurs 10s; 5 horses £14; one saddle, one bridle 5s; one brass pot 10s; in pewter 3s 4d; one chest 10s; 3 standing beds 30s; one feather bed, one bolster, one blanket, one covering, for a board, one coverlet 30s; one beef tub 6s 8d; 2 chairs 2s; one long table in the hall & forms 40s; one caliver, one head-piece, one flax and touchbox 10s; milk boards and shelves 3s 4d; one 'Rakentyth' [?chain] 8d; one table in the kitchen, one dishboard, one cheese-press and one other board 10s; one old chest 3s; 12 sapling boards & other woods in the chamber over the kitchen 13s 4d; one other 'Rackenteth' & bulk, 18d; one board clog [?] 20d; one corn wain chest & one muckwain chest 13s 4d; in wheels 7s 8d; one great ark in the barn 40s; one turf wain 6s 8d; 8 pieces of wood in the barn 5s; one tugwithy 10d; one plough & coulter 2s; two staples & two rings, two oxen yokes & one wimble 20d; two swine troughs 20d. [Total] £37.

5. John Weever, gent. (16 February, 1632; proved 29 March 1632). PCC.

In Dei nomine Amen. I, John Weever of the parish of St James Clerkenwell in the county of Middlesex, gent., being in sound mind and perfect health of body, thanks be to almighty God, do make and ordain this my last will and testament in manner and form following. Imprimis, I commit my soul into the hands of the almighty, omnipotent and everliving God, in full assurance of everlasting salvation through the merits, death and passion of his only begotten Son, Jesus Christ, my alone saviour and redeemer. As for my body, I commit the same to Christian burial expecting a joyful resurrection. And for and concerning such worldly estate as God hath blessed me withal, I bequeath the same in manner and form following. Item, I give and bequeath unto my brother William Weever my black cloak with many laces. Item, I give to my sister Alice Cawthorne twenty shillings. Item, I give to my sister Anne Caton twenty shillings. Item, to my sister Isabel Holt twenty shillings. All which said several legacies to be given and paid to my brother and three sisters as aforesaid, my will is shall be given and paid by Anne my dearly beloved wife within one year next after my decease. And I do make and ordain my said wife Anne Weever the sole executrix of this my last will and testament. And I do make and appoint my nephew William Cawthorne overseer of this my will, to whom I give twenty shillings to buy him a ring. Item, I give and bequeath my lease of my house in Gray's Inn Lane, now in the tenure of George Dawson, and the lease of my house in Clerkenwell wherein I now dwell, together with all goods, chattels, moneys, plate, household stuff and all the rest of my personal estate whatsoever, not before bequeathed, to my said executrix Anne Weever, my beloved wife. And lastly I do hereby revoke and make void all former wills and testaments by me made. In witness whereof I have hereto set my hand and seal the sixteenth day of February in the seventh year of the reign of our sovereign lord Charles, by the grace of God King of England, Scotland, France and Ireland, defender of the faith &c Annoque Domini one thousand six hundred thirty one John Weever. Signed and sealed in the presence of John Witt and Wm. Gardner.

# Appendix B. *Genealogical tables*

## (1) *Hoghton of Hoghton Tower*

(Based on a pedigree at Hoghton Tower; *A Short Guide to Hoghton Tower*; *The History of Preston* (1900), by Henry Fishwick.)

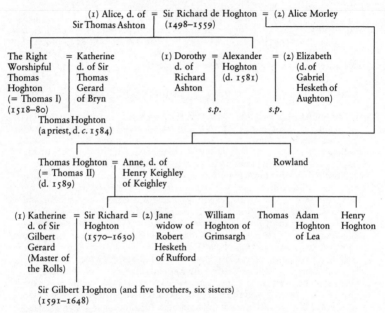

N.B. (1) In this and the following tables I have simplified by omitting some younger brothers and sisters, and childless wives.

(2) Sir Richard de Hoghton, who married four times, also had many illegitimate children. These included Leonard, Richard, Richard the younger (later known as Richard of Park Hall: cf. p. 10 above), Gilbert, Arthur, George, and at least two daughters (Elizabeth, wife of Robert Talbot (cf. p. 140, above), and another Elizabeth). See Lumby, *Calendar*, no. 1410 and Index, and Miller, *Hoghton Tower*, p. 149.

(3) Thomas, the son of Thomas I, has caused some confusion. John Talbot, Thomas Barton, Bartholomew Hesketh and other Hoghton friends testified on 30 July 1580 that Thomas I died without 'heirs male of his body', and that Alexander Hoghton 'is living at Lea' and is his brother (Lumby, *Calendar*, no. 50). But Thomas I is thought to have had a son, Thomas, a priest (who was therefore an outlaw, so could not be an heir), who died in Salford gaol *c.* 1584: that may explain why Thomas II sought an exemplification that he was the lawful heir in Feb. 1584 (Lumby, *Cal.*, no. 1407).

# Appendix B

## (2) *Butler of Middle Rawcliffe*

(Based on Henry Fishwick, *The History of the Parish of St Michaels-on-Wyre, CS,* 1891, XXV, p. 159.)

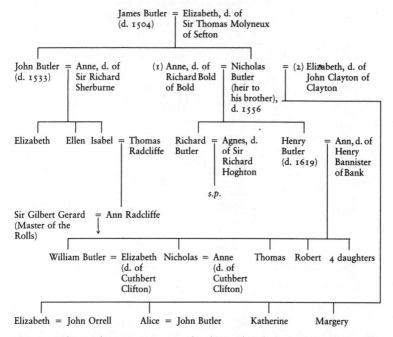

N.B. (1) Either Katherine or Margery, daughters of Nicholas Butler and Elizabeth Clayton, could have been the mother of *John Weever* (the nephew of Henry Butler); but Weever could also have been the son of an unrecorded daughter or illegitimate daughter of Nicholas Butler.

(2) Sir Gilbert Gerard and Ann Radcliffe were the parents of Sir Thomas Gerard, dedicatee of Weever's *Epigrammes,* and of the three sisters who married three other dedicatees (Sir Richard Hoghton, Sir Richard Molyneux, Sir Peter Leigh): cf. p. 51.

## (3) *Cottam (Cottom) of Tarnacre*

(Based on *Visitation 1613*, and on Chapter IV, above.)

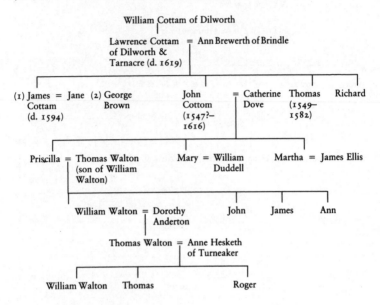

William Cottam of Dilworth

Lawrence Cottam = Ann Brewerth of Brindle
of Dilworth &
Tarnacre (d. 1619)

(1) James = Jane (2) George    John = Catherine  Thomas   Richard
Cottam          Brown         Cottom    Dove   (1549–
(d. 1594)                     (1547?–          1582)
                              1616)

Priscilla = Thomas Walton    Mary = William    Martha = James Ellis
            (son of William         Duddell
            Walton)

William Walton = Dorothy    John    James    Ann
                 Anderton

Thomas Walton = Anne Hesketh
                of Turneaker

William Walton   Thomas             Roger

# Appendix B

## (4) Salusbury of Lleweni and Rug

(Based on *Calendar of Salusbury Correspondence 1553 – circa 1700*, ed. W. J. Smith (Cardiff, 1954); and Brown, *Salusbury and Chester*.)

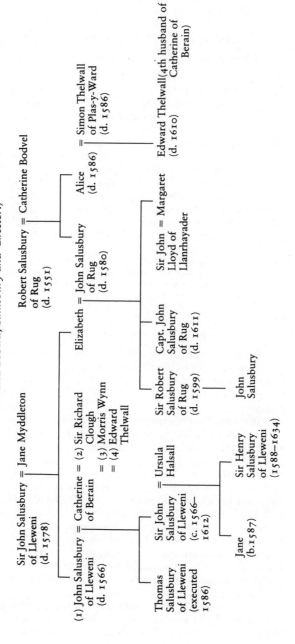

[149]

## Appendix C. *A Midsummer Night's Dream,*
## *Henry VI* Parts 2 and 3, and the Stanley family

After suggesting that Shakespeare served for some years as one of Lord Strange's Men, I noted that he seems to have rearranged history in *Richard III*, giving a more flattering picture than did the chronicles of his patrons' ancestor, the first Earl of Derby; and that he brought Lord Strange more prominently into *Love's Labour's Lost*, his most topical comedy, than previous commentators have suspected (cf. p. 63ff.). *A Midsummer Night's Dream* is a third play with possible Derby connections. Editors have repeated, with remarkable unanimity, that this comedy must have been written – or adapted – for an important wedding, preferably one attended by Queen Elizabeth. The elaborate compliment in II.1.157 ff. would have had a particular relish if the Queen herself, 'in maiden meditation, fancy-free', graced the bridal celebrations. Cupid, we hear, took aim

> At a fair vestal throned by the west,
> And loosed his love-shaft smartly from his bow
> As it should pierce a hundred thousand hearts;
> But I might see young Cupid's fiery shaft
> Quenched in the chaste beams of the watery moon;
> And the imperial votaress passed on
> In maiden meditation, fancy-free.

The Queen attended a number of weddings in the 1590s but, as E. K. Chambers and others have shown, the effective choice lies between two: either (1) that of William, sixth Earl of Derby and Elizabeth Vere at Greenwich on 26 January 1595; or (2) that of Thomas Berkeley and Elizabeth Carey at Blackfriars on 19 February 1596. Shakespeare and his colleagues would have a reason for making a special effort on each occasion: (1) the sixth Earl of Derby was a brother of Ferdinando, Lord Strange, who had been the patron of several leading members of the company from *c.* 1586 till 1594 (cf. p. 59); (2) Elizabeth Carey was a granddaughter of Lord Hunsdon, the Lord Chamberlain who was patron of the company in February 1596. The Queen was present at the Derby wedding, and, since the bride was her god-daughter, may well have attended Elizabeth Carey's as well. Chambers and Harold Brooks, the New Arden editor, both favour (2) as the occasion for which *Dream* was composed but admit that the choice between the two weddings is not an easy one. 'Either wedding', said Chambers, 'would fit such indications of date as the play yields'.[1] Believing as I do that Chambers post-dated many of Shakespeare's early plays,[2] I think that more can and should be said for the earlier of the two most likely dates – the marriage of William, sixth Earl of Derby.

(1) 'The much-travelled Theseus might have been thought appropriate to William Stanley, whose own travels are said to have taken him as far as the Holy Land and Russia' (E. K. Chambers[3]). Even if William Stanley never

reached the Holy Land and Russia, as sceptics have alleged, he certainly travelled abroad for some years.[4] (2) William Stanley was keenly interested in poetry and drama; he kept his own company of players, and, a few years after his marriage, in 1599, was said to be 'busy penning comedies for the common players'.[5] Shakespeare's Theseus similarly takes a special interest in poetry and drama. These two possible allusions have been pointed out before, but there are additional reasons for connecting Theseus and Earl William. (3) The Earl married late, compared with his contemporaries: he was born between 1560 and 1562,[6] and would be in his thirties when he married in 1595. (His brother, Ferdinando, was born *c.* 1559 and married in 1579.) This, again, connects him with Theseus, a 'mature' bridegroom in the play. (4) It is a curious coincidence that, of the three marriages that are the strongest contenders as the 'occasion' of *A Midsummer Night's Dream*, one and only one fits in with what appears to be a topical allusion in the play's opening speeches.

> Now, fair Hippolyta, our nuptial hour
> Draws on apace; four happy days bring in
> Another moon; but, O, methinks, how slow
> This old moon wanes! ...
> Four days will quickly steep themselves in night;
> Four nights will quickly dream away the time;
> And then the moon, like to a silver bow
> New bent in heaven, shall behold the night
> Of our solemnities.

Could the four days be a clue to the play's date? Find out moonshine, find out moonshine! According to H. H. Goldstine's tables of new and full moons,[7] there was a new moon on 30 January 1595, exactly four days after Earl William's wedding; and Goldstine also tells us that new moons appeared on 18 February 1596 (one day before the Berkeley–Carey marriage) and on 10 May 1594 (eight days after the Heneage–Southampton marriage, to which I shall return in a moment). It is true that the play proclaims that the marriage itself will coincide with a new moon; as I suggested in dealing with 'Ferdinand' in *Love's Labour's Lost*, however, dramatists had to be careful not to mirror contemporary great ones too obviously (cf. p. 69). If *Dream* was performed on a wedding-day, as is usually assumed, the emphatic statement that a new moon is due in precisely four days, which happened to be true on 26 January 1595, would alert spectators to expect other topical allusions, and that would be as far as it would be prudent to go. For the play is not a *roman à clef*, and Theseus is not Earl William, though there are teasing similarities. It would, of course, have been a simple matter to add the play's nineteen opening lines as it neared completion, when the exact date of this long-awaited marriage was at last decided.

The date of the Derby wedding, by the way, is given by Stowe. 'The 26 of January William Earl of Derby married the Earl of Oxford's daughter at the court then at Greenwich, which marriage feast was there most royally kept.' Chambers pointed out that a different date seems to be indicated by the churchwardens' accounts of St Martin's Westminster, for 1595: 'Item, paid the 30th of January for ringing at her Majesty's coming to the Lord Treasurer's to the Earl of Derby's wedding, and at her departure from thence the first of February, 2s'. Chambers added that such bell-ringings 'are often entered with only approximate accuracy',[8] but his argument for preferring Stowe's date seems to me not proven, especially since he concedes that Stowe was wrong as to the place of the wedding. The later date would fit in pleasingly with the play's emphasis that the Theseus wedding will coincide with a new moon; whichever date turns out to be the correct one, however – 26 or 30 January 1595 – it looks as if the 'new moon' lines contain a topical allusion. And this is confirmed by (5), the description of Theseus' impatience –

> but, O, methinks how slow
> This old moon wanes! She lingers my desires
> Like to a step-dame or a dowager
> Long withering out a young man's revenue.

Earl William's wedding had to be deferred for some months, Ferdinando's widow being pregnant when he died. Had the dowager Countess of Derby given birth to a son, Earl William would have been 'unearled', and his long-expected marriage would have been stopped. Earl William wrote impatiently about these delays in September 1594,[9] and might well have thought that a *dowager* lingered his desires and 'withered out' his revenue. The lawsuits of Ferdinando's widow and daughters against Earl William dragged on for years, and it must have become obvious in the months preceding the earl's wedding that they would. (Ferdinando's widow married Thomas Egerton, the Lord Keeper and later Lord Chancellor, in 1600. We know from Egerton's private papers that she was a strong-willed and difficult woman: he complained of her greed, extravagance and ill-temper, her 'cursed railing and bitter tongue'.[10] If Shakespeare alluded unkindly to his former master's widow, as I suggest, there are good reasons for believing that she deserved it.)

(6) Once we are alerted to the possibility that Theseus may be an idealised portrait of Earl William, other passages in the play, that have not been seen as 'topical' by previous commentators, need to be scanned afresh. For example, Theseus' pride in his hunting-dogs:

> My hounds are bred out of the Spartan kind,
> So flewed, so sanded; and their heads are hung
> With ears that sweep away the morning dew;
> Crook-kneed and dew-lapped like Thessalian bulls;
> Slow in pursuit, but matched in mouth like bells. (IV.1.106 ff.)

It has long been a belief, wrote F. A. Bailey, 'in which so great an authority as J. H. Round concurred [*Peerage and Pedigree* (1910), II, 32–5], that the original Stanley coat ... may have owed its three stags' heads to a fortunate marriage with an heiress, Joan, daughter of Philipe de Bamvile, in the late thirteenth century; this was, in Round's estimation, 'the turning point in the history of the family', for Joan brought to the Stanleys (hitherto of Stafford-shire) the lordship of Storeton and the hereditary office of Master Forester of Wirral in Cheshire'.[11] The Earls of Derby kept the three stags' heads in their coat of arms. Theseus, to be sure, was a famous huntsman – yet his speech about his marvellous dogs has an air of being there for its own sake. And what would be more natural than that the Master Forester kept his own hounds, and was proud of them? We know that the Leighs of Lyme, who were Deputy Stewards of the forest of Macclesfield under the Earls of Derby, maintained a celebrated breed of Lyme mastiffs, and perhaps Shakespeare referred to these (the Earls of Derby addressed the Leighs of Lyme as their 'servants'), or to others like them – hounds that may well have been present at the Derby wedding.

I now return to two other topical allusions that have been discussed before. (7) The play seems to refer to an episode at the Scottish court in August 1594, described in *A True Reportarie* (S.R., 24 October 1594). While King James was at dinner, a chariot was drawn in by a Moor. 'This chariot should have been drawn in by a lion, but because his presence might have brought some fear to the nearest ... it was thought meet that the Moor should supply that room.' 'Bottom and his fellows', said Harold Brooks, 'likewise planning a performance before their sovereign, anticipate the fear that bringing in "a lion among ladies" may produce, and likewise modify their plan in order to avoid it.'[12] Though Shakespeare might still refer back to this episode in 1596, a joke about something that happened four hundred miles from London would lose its savour more quickly than one concerned with local events; Earl William's marriage in January 1595, would come at the right time for such an allusion, the 1596 marriage less so. (8) 'The bad weather described in II.1.81–117 is probably that which began in March, 1594, prevailed during the greater part of that year, and ushered in a long period of corn shortage' (E. K. Chambers). It is noteworthy that the bad weather extended over four seasons –

> The spring, the summer,
> The childing autumn, angry winter, change
> Their wonted liveries

– not only because four seasons bring us precisely to the period of Earl William's marriage in January 1595, but also because this allusion rules out another possible marriage, that of Sir Thomas Heneage and Mary, Countess of Southampton, on 2 May 1594. The Countess's son, the Earl of Southampton, was another patron whom Shakespeare might wish to please at this time, and Sir Thomas was a 'mature' bridegroom (aged sixty-two or so in 1594), but, as we have seen, quite apart from the weather the 'new moon' eliminates this marriage, and no one now presses its claims.

While I am primarily concerned with Shakespeare and Lord Strange (the fifth Earl), the possibility that he also wrote *A Midsummer Night's Dream* for the sixth Earl's wedding, when he was no longer officially attached to the Stanleys, deserves a place in our story. For if Theseus gives us an idealised portrait of Earl William it follows that Shakespeare's two most obviously topical plays, *Love's Labour's Lost* and *A Midsummer Night's Dream*, were written for the same family, and this would be additional proof – if more is needed – of the dramatist's very special relationship with the brilliant Ferdinando, Lord Strange.

Let us now turn to *Henry VI, Parts 2 and 3*, where the dramatist tampered with history as in *Richard III*, though not quite so transparently. It has long been recognised that in his account of the Wars of the Roses Shakespeare leaned towards Lancaster (and the 'Lancashire connection' that I have outlined may help to explain this bias). Why, we may ask, did he magnify the achievements or sufferings of some individuals, while he left others more or less as he found them? Was it because of a general prejudice in favour of Lancaster, or could there have been a more particular reason? The emphasis given to the deaths of Lord Clifford and of his son (2 *Henry VI*, V.1.122–216, V.2.1–65; 3 *Henry VI*, II.6.1–86) is a case in point. Geoffrey Bullough said of the second that 'the prolonged ill-treatment of [young Clifford's] corpse was intended to illustrate the growing cruelty of the civil war';[13] and Kenneth Muir has suggested that young Clifford's speech on discovering his father's body (2 *Henry VI*, V.2.31–56) is stylistically more mature than the rest of the play, and has left no trace in the reported text or 'bad quarto' – that is, was an afterthought.[14] We may think that the highlighting of the Clifford scenes, and Shakespeare's retouching of some of the material, needs no justification other than that it adds to dramatic balance. It is worth bearing in mind, however, that Ferdinando, Lord Strange, was the son of Margaret Clifford, and was therefore a direct descendant of the Cliffords represented in *Henry VI*; also, that Ferdinando's 'Stanley' ancestors had not yet risen to prominence in the reign of Henry VI – if Lord Strange was to have the pleasure of identifying himself with any of the principal figures in Shakespeare's version of history it had to be through his mother's family. That could explain why Shakespeare inserted what is in effect a 'Clifford sequence' in *Henry VI*, exalting young Clifford as one of the most resolute champions of the house of Lancaster, and attempting to account for the killing of Rutland and York by showing that these brutalities all resulted from young Clifford's devotion to his elderly father, and horror on discovering his father's mangled body.

> Wast thou ordained, dear father,
> To lose thy youth in peace, and to achieve
> The silver livery of advised age,
> And, in thy reverence and thy chair-days, thus
> To die in ruffian battle?
> (2 *Henry VI*, V.2.45–9)

The chronicles are silent about old Clifford's age, merely mentioning him as one of the many who fell at the battle of St Albans. We know that 'old' Clifford was 41 when he died, but Shakespeare made him a much older man, 'in thy reverence and thy chair-days', and thus increased young Clifford's outrage and thirst for revenge.

Whether Shakespeare saw from the outset that young Clifford's killing of Rutland and York had to be prepared for, or added young Clifford's speech over his father's body as an 'afterthought', is not easy to prove. I think, though, that the absence of this speech from the reported text must be related to the text's origins. The purpose of the speech is to prepare for the sequel, 3 *Henry VI*. If 2 *Henry VI* and 3 *Henry VI* were performed consecutively, the speech is needed; if, however, 2 *Henry VI* was performed on its own when the reported text came into being, such a long preparatory speech would be less functional and might well be dropped, since it obstructs the 'closure' of 2 *Henry VI* in its dying moments.

# Notes

## Preface to the first edition

1 See Baker, *In Shakespeare's Warwickshire*, and Chambers, *Gleanings* ('William Shakeshafte'). Chambers had noted the existence of William Shakeshafte in 1923 (*Stage*, I, 280, n.) but, as Harold Jenkins points out to me, did not connect Shakeshafte and Shakespeare before Baker did so in 1937.

## I. Introduction

1 T. W. Baldwin points out (*Small Latine*, I, 487) that, while some theorists said that a boy ought to be ready to go to university at fifteen, the available statistics show that some went earlier and many later. Between 1567 and 1579, 40 went to Oxford at 12 years of age, 56 at 13, 115 at 14, 135 at 15, 193 at 16, 247 at 17, 306 at 18, 198 at 19, 144 at 20. This suggests that 16 or 17 would be a more usual age to leave school than 15.

2 Chambers, *Shakespeare*, II, 252. As Chambers explains (I, 17), '"killing a calf" seems to have been an item in the repertory of wandering entertainers'; it could be that Aubrey and others misunderstood this phrase when they said that Shakespeare worked as a butcher's apprentice.

3 Schoenbaum, *Documentary Life*, 27.

4 See Leslie Hotson, *Shakespeare's Sonnets Dated*, p. 231, and below, p. 118.

5 See Baldwin, *op. cit.*, I, 464: 'the King's free Grammar School at Stratford.'

6 I, 480 ff.

## II. Hoghton of Hoghton Tower

1 J. H. Lumby indexed the most important documents in *A Calendar of the Deeds and Papers in the possession of Sir James de Hoghton, Bart.* (1936). The DDHo Index at the LRO 'relates to documents deposited by Sir Cuthbert de Hoghton, Bart., in addition to those in the Calendar published by [Lumby]. Presented to the County Council, 1953.' Sir Bernard de Hoghton still has many strong-boxes filled with undeposited (mainly eighteenth- and nineteenth-century) deeds and papers, which were recently moved from the estate office to Hoghton Tower.

2 BL, Harleian MS. 7386, fo. 290b; see also Miller, *Hoghton Tower*, p. 101. Miller's book contains many illustrations of Hoghton Tower, pedigrees, etc., and is most useful, though sometimes unreliable.

3 Miller, *op. cit.*, p. 168; cf. J. Gillow, *English Catholics*, III, 328.

4 Lumby, *Calendar*, no. 1393; BL, Add. MS. 32,106 fo. 131.

5 Add. MS. 32,106 fo. 132b.

6 Add. MS. 32,106; PRO, DL4 48 (49).

7 Quoted from J. Gillow, *The Haydock Papers: a Glimpse into English Catholic Life* (1888), p. 10 ff.; Miller (*Hoghton Tower*, p. 74) calls the author of the ballad Roger Anderson.

8 Gillow, *op. cit.*, p. 15.

9 *APC*, XIII, 149.

10 *APC*, XIII, 290.

11 W. D. Selby, *Lancashire and Cheshire Records Preserved in the Public Record Office, London* (RSLC, 1882, vol. VII), II, 342.
12 Gillow, *Haydock Papers*, 9, 17.
13 *APC*, XII, 346.
14 See Lumby, *Calendar*, no. 1406; Miller (*Hoghton Tower*, p. 158) calls it Ashton Hall.
15 DL1 125 (H3); Selby, *op. cit.*, II, 279; DL4 25 (27).
16 *SPD*, 229.25; BL, Add. MS. 32,106, p. 206.
17 *SPD*, 241.52.
18 *Lancashire Funeral Certificates*, ed. T. W. King (CS, vol. 75), 1869, p. 66.
19 See Lumby, *Calendar*, no. 52.
20 J. Gillow, 'The Catholic Registers of Salwick and Lea in the Fylde' (CRS, XV, 155).
21 *The Letters of John Chamberlain*, ed. N. E. McClure (2 vols., Philadelphia, 1939), I, 75.
22 *SPD*, 226.18; HMC, Hatfield House, X, 30.
23 HMC, Hatfield House,'X, 343–4.
24 DDIn 47 (2).
25 Miller, *Hoghton Tower*, 87–8; cf. Lumby, *Calendar*, no. 54.
26 See Douglas Hamer, 'Was William Shakespeare William Shakeshafte?' (RES, 1970, XXI, 41–8).
27 E. K. Chambers, *Sources for a Biography of Shakespeare* (Oxford, 1946), p. 11.
28 Privately communicated.
29 Cf. p. 13.
30 Chambers, *Shakespeare*, II, 372.
31 See Mark Eccles, *Shakespeare in Warwickshire* (Madison, Wis., 1961), p. 7.
32 Eccles, p. 11.
33 *Henslowe's Diary*, p. 273.
34 *APC*, XIII, 269 (3 Dec. 1581).
35 The entries in the *Household Book* (DDF 2429) are written in a difficult hand, which is sometimes a form of shorthand. The last letters of many words are simply squiggles.
36 *SPD*, 240.138.
37 See William Beamont, *Winwick* (Warrington, 1878), p. 75, for Mather; A. L. Rowse, *Sex and Society in Shakespeare's Age Simon Forman the Astrologer* (1974), p. 276 ff.; E. C. Gaskell, *The Life of Charlotte Bronte* (ed. 1858), p. 30 ff.
38 *SPD*, 243.52.
39 See Add. MS. 32,106, no. 379; Henry Fishwick, *The History of the Parish of Preston* (1900), p. 260 ff.
40 PRO, *Calendarium Inquis. post Mortem*.
41 See *The Stanley Papers*, Part II, p. lxxiii.
42 Cf. Leatherbarrow, *Elizabethan Recusants*, p. 55 etc.
43 Joseph Gillow, *Lord Burghley's Map of Lancashire in 1590*, 1907, p. 1; cf. Christopher Haigh, *Reformation and Resistance in Tudor Lancashire* (Cambridge, 1975).
44 A typescript owned by Sir Bernard de Hoghton, Bt.
45 G. C. Miller, *Hoghton Tower*, pp. 154–5.
46 Gillow, *English Catholics*, III, 327. Not all of the Hoghtons supported Catholic education, of course. Sir Gilbert (son of Sir Richard) became a Governor of Blackburn Grammar School, at the early age of twenty (Miller, *Hoghton Tower*, pp. 174–5).
47 William Beamont, *A History of the House of Lyme* (Warrington, 1876), p. 93; *The House of Lyme* by Lady Newton (1917), p. 43.
48 Cf. Lumby, *Calendar*, no. 1409: 'the manors of English Lea and French Lea commonly known as the Lea'.

49 Baker, *In Shakespeare's Warwickshire*, p. 303.
50 Lumby, *Calendar*, no. 1396.
51 Ed. 1882, 3 vols, I, 574.
52 Cf. Baker, *op. cit.*, and Chambers, *Gleanings*.
53 Miller, p. 158.

## III. Sir Thomas Hesketh of Rufford

1 In this paragraph I am indebted to *Rufford Old Hall* (The National Trust, 1979), p. 32.
2 Alan Keen and Roger Lubbock, *The Annotator*, p. 46.
3 L. Hotson, *Shakespeare's Sonnets Dated* (1949), pp. 128–9.
4 *HSLC*(1908), LIX, 93 ff.
5 *Mary Lyvesey v. Thomas Houghton* (DL4, 25 Eliz.); DDHe 6.19; DDHe 18.26; Add. MS. 32,104 fo. 32b.
6 See Add. MS. 32,104 fo. 352.
7 Procter, p. 107.
8 Dame Alice Hesketh's will, in the LRO, is dated 20 November 1604.
9 *Rufford Old Hall* (The National Trust, 1979), pp. 14–15.

## IV. John Cottom of Tarnacre

1 T. W. Baldwin, *Small Latine*, I, chap. xxii.
2 DL1 227 (62); DL4 52 (30).
3 BL, Add. MS. 32,115 (C 162).
4 DL4 52 (30).
5 This may be the Edward Gregson who made his will on 8 May 1607, and bequeathed 'to his master Henry Butler, Esq., and his wife, either of them, £5. He gives to Nicholas Butler [their son] £5' (abstract in Add. MS. 32,115 (G63)). If so, this helps to show that John Weever's uncle, Henry Butler, and the Cottom family must have known each other.
6 See also *Quarter Sessions*, ed. James Tait, pp. 128, 147, 157.
7 DDH 710; cf. DDCl 916.
8 BL, Add. MS. 32,115 (H 149).
9 DL4 48 (49).
10 Cf. the long list of 'Debts owing to me George Duddell ... 1589', endorsed 'This is a true copy of the debitory' (DDF 1241).
11 DDIn 64 (74 and 75).
12 BL, Add. MS. 32,115 (D89).
13 DL1 153.
14 DL1 168.
15 DDCl 142, 208.
16 PCC; cf. also *The Stanley Papers*, Part II, pp. 24, 84: William Doddill served the Earl of Derby as Yeoman of the Pantries (1587) and Groom of the Chamber (1590).
17 BL, Add. MS. 32,115 (D52).
18 York wills (Borthwick Institute), vol. 28, fo. 708.
19 *SPD*, 275.64.

## V. John Weever and the Hoghtons

1 For Henry Bannister of Bank and Sir Thomas Hesketh see DL4 26 (29); DL4 26 (83); DL1 125 (H 14); DDHe 19 (5). In DDHe 6 (11) Henry Bannister is a witness for Sir Thomas (1584).

2 I assume that Robert Dalton of Pilling, Esq., was also Robert Dalton of Thurnham, Esq., just as Alexander Hoghton was 'of Lea' and also of 'Hoghton Tower', and Sir Thomas Hesketh was 'of Rufford' and also 'of Holmswood'. Weever included a verse epistle 'to the author's most honoured friend, *Richard Dalton of Pilling*' in his *Mirror of Martyrs* (1601); Richard here may be a misprint for Robert.

3 McKerrow, in his edition of Weever's *Epigrammes*, almost certainly misidentified Sir Thomas Gerard as 'of Bryn, in Lancashire' (who was also related to the Hoghtons). Sir Gilbert Gerard's son, Sir Thomas, was the Knight Marshal; see HMC, Hatfield House, XI, 109; 'the letters which Sir Thomas Garrat, K. Marshall, wrote to his brother in law, Sir R. Mull.' (=Mullineux); XI, 160 (Sir R. Molyneux to Cecil, 1601: 'Not long ago you delivered to my brother [i.e. brother-in-law] Sir Tho. Gerrard, to be sent to me, a letter'). According to Hasler, Sir Thomas Gerard became knight marshal of the Household in 1597.

4 'Honey-tongued Shakespeare' was also Meres's phrase (quoted above, p. 54). Did Weever simply repeat Meres? That would help us to date Weever's sonnet (*Palladis Tamia* was entered in the S.R. on 7 Sept. 1598); *OED*, however, first records 'honey-tongued' in *Love's Labour's Lost*, V.2.334, and by 1598 this word may have been in common use. For *tainted* (l. 3) read *tinted*. Weever's 'rosecheek'd Adonis' (l. 5) quotes *Venus and Adonis*, l. 3. And, as A. Davenport noted, Weever re-used l. 10 in *Faunus and Melliflora* (1600): 'And thus fair words and power attractive beauty / Bring men to women in subjective duty' (ed. Davenport, 1948, p. 17). Presumably Weever meant 'power-attractive'. According to McKerrow 'the word "het" in l. 13 means "heated".' I would paraphrase lines 13–14 as follows: 'They [i.e. the thousands entranced by Shakespeare's characters] burn in love; thy children [characters] heated them. Go, woo thy muse, and beget more beautiful children [brood, *OED*, 1c] for them!'

5 Eleven leaves survive from a lost edition of *Passionate Pilgrim*, which is tentatively dated 1599 (cf. *A Short-Title Catalogue . . . 1475–1640*, revised edition (ed. W. A. Jackson, F. S. Ferguson, K. Pantzer), *before* the first complete edition of 1599.

6 I assume that Weever's text of *Epigrammes* was not properly 'finalised', and that, being an inexperienced author, he expected the printer to tidy it as instructed; the printer, however, was more anxious to finish quickly (hence the large quota of misprints). Another sign that Weever did not check through his text before it was printed occurs in the heading of vi.1, 'Ad Richardum Houghton Militem': dedication i, to 'Sir Richard Houghton', shows that the book came out after Hoghton was knighted in June 1599.

7 The date of Weever's sonnet depends on 'honey-tongued Shakespeare' (cf. note 4, above). If Weever echoed Meres, he probably wrote his sonnet in the autumn or winter of 1598; if not, in 1597 or 1598. Interestingly, Weever only names works already printed (*Venus and Adonis*, *Lucrece*, *Romeo*, and either *Richard III* or *Richard II*: all printed by 1597); he could have written his sonnet while a student at Cambridge, before he had seen one of the plays in the theatre.

8 See A. Davenport, ed. *The Whipping of the Satyre* (Liverpool, 1951).

9 *Ben Jonson* (ed. C. H. Herford, P. and E. Simpson, 11 vols, Oxford, 1925–52), VIII, 32. The quotation from *Every Man In His Humour* differs in the Quarto and Folio texts.

10 *Op. cit.*, p. 27.

11 Weever, p. 279. Halle's *Chronicle* says that the heads were fixed on poles, and that Cade 'caused them in every street [to] kiss together' (*2 Henry VI*, New Arden ed., p. 170).

12 *Ancient Funeral Monuments*, p. 234. Weever refers to the son of Sir Richard Hoghton's brother-in-law.

13 Henry Butler's will was printed by G. J. Piccope (*Lancashire and Cheshire Wills and Inventories*, Third Portion, CS, 1861, p. 182). Ann Butler, Henry's widow,

# Notes

died in 1622, and a 'note' of her bequests survives in the LRO, made out by her son Thomas.

## VI. Shakespeare and Lord Strange's Men

1 Cf. p. 4.
2 Cf. Chambers, *Stage*, II, 123, 197–8.
3 W. W. Greg thought Strange's Men alone acted *Seven Deadly Sins*, Part 2 (*Henslowe Papers*, ed. Greg, 1907, p. 129); Chambers (*Stage*, II, 120) thought that Strange's men could have combined with Admiral's Men.
4 Cf. Andrew Gurr, *The Shakespearean Stage* (Cambridge, 1970), p. 69.
5 Chambers, *Stage*, II, 128.
6 Honigmann, *Shakespeare's Impact on his Contemporaries* (1982), p. 53 ff.
7 P. Alexander, *Shakespeare's 'Henry VI' and 'Richard III'* (Cambridge, 1929).
8 II, 130.
9 Chambers, *Stage*, IV, 347–8.
10 *Stage*, II, 129.
11 *Stage*, II, 130.
12 I am aware that it has also been suggested that Shakespeare began his career with the Queen's Men. See G. M. Pinciss, *Shakespeare Survey* (1974), XXVII, 129–36; S. McMillin, *RES* (1976), XXVII, 174–7.
13 *Stage*, II, 128.
14 Abel Lefranc and Alan Keen both argued that Shakespeare remodelled events in *Richard III* because of his connection with the Stanley family, anticipating some of my points in this paragraph (*Sous le Masque*, I, 244 ff.; *The Annotator*, pp. 84–5).
15 Barry Coward states that '*Sans Changer*' was adopted 'by the fourth and fifth earls of Derby in the sixteenth century along with the motto '*Dieu et ma Foy*' (*The Stanleys*, p. 15, n. 3). Ferdinando, however, had the motto '*Sans changer ma vérité*' inscribed in his portrait: cf. *The Stanley Papers*, Part 2, p. lxv; *The Annotator*, Plate V.
16 Cf. Honigmann, *Shakespeare's Impact*, p. 139, n. 37.
17 See F. P. Wilson's Supplement to McKerrow's *Nashe*, V, 15–16.
18 Chapman, letter to M. Roydon prefixed to *The Shadow of Night*.
19 Lord Strange was descended (through his mother, Margaret Clifford) from Mary, the younger sister of Henry VIII, and was therefore seen as a possible successor to Queen Elizabeth.
20 *The Stanley Papers*, Part 2, p. v.
21 *Love's Labour's Lost*, ed. R. David, p. xxxi.
22 Greene's *Groat's Worth of Wit* (1592).
23 See my articles in *MLR* (1954), XLIX, 293–307; *The Library* (1982), IV, 142–73; and in *The New York Review of Books* (1984), XXXI, 16–18.
24 See *Henslowe's Diary*, p. 16 ff.
25 Chambers, *Shakespeare*, II, 188.
26 Chambers, *loc. cit.*
27 Chambers, *Shakespeare*, II, 219.
28 Chambers, *Shakespeare*, II, 186.
29 *Shakespeare's Impact*, p. 135.
30 Chambers, *Shakespeare*, II, 189.
31 *Shakespeare's Impact*, p. 74.
32 Cf. Chambers, *Stage*, IV, 229–33; Honigmann, '*John a Kent* and Marprelate' (*Yearbook of English Studies*, 1983, XIII, 288–93). It should be noted that, while there is a good deal of support for 1589–90 as the date of *Tears of the Muses*, the poem is sometimes dated earlier.

33 Honigmann, *Shakespeare's Impact*, chap. I.
34 Chambers, *Shakespeare*, II, 214. My italics.
35 Cf. A. C. Judson, *The Life of Edmund Spenser* (Baltimore, 1945), p. 160.
36 Chambers, *Shakespeare*, II, 245.
37 Judson, *op. cit.*, p. 146.
38 Alfred Harbage also thought that 'pleasant Willy' and 'Aetion' referred to Shakespeare (*Shakespeare Without Words and other Essays*, Cambridge, Mass., 1972, pp. 139–41).

## VII. The Shakespeare epitaphs and the Stanleys

1 See Chambers, *Shakespeare*, II, 268–9; I, 551 ff.; and Schoenbaum, 'Shakespeare's Epitaphs' (in *Lives*, 1970, pp. 75–82).
2 See Chambers, *Shakespeare*, I, 550; II, 140; I, 554.
3 Hotson, *Shakespeare's Sonnets Dated* (1949), pp. 111 ff., 134.
4 *Shakespeare Encyclopaedia*, p. 821; so Schoenbaum (as in n. 1, above), p. 78.
5 PPC (110 Wingfield).
6 D. N. Durant, *Bess of Hardwick* (1977), p. 200.
7 *Ancient Funeral Monuments*, p. 18.
8 According to the Victoria County History, there is a Leigh chapel in Winwick church, and Sir Peter Leigh re-founded Winwick Grammar School in 1619 (*Lancashire*, IV, 124, 130).
9 Chambers, *Shakespeare*, I, 553.
10 DL4 26 (18).
11 PCC (39 Carew). Sir Thomas was 'in trouble' in 1571 when he tried to rescue Mary Queen of Scots, and was imprisoned in the Tower for his pains.
12 PCC (92 Drake).
13 See Chambers, *Shakespeare*, II, 246–7, 181.
14 Chambers, *op. cit.*, II, 259.
15 Cf. Chambers, *op. cit.*, II, 181.
16 Chambers, *op. cit.*, II, 153.

## VIII. Thomas Savage of Rufford

1 *Shakespeare Encyclopaedia*, p. 736.
2 *Lives*, p. 746.
3 Her will is in the Lancashire Record Office.
4 *The Registers of the Parish Church of Croston in the County of Lancaster*, ed. Henry Fishwick (Wigan: Lancashire Parish Register Society, 1900), I, 124.
5 Minute Book, I, 47.
6 See Savage's will, Appendix A, p. 143, and above, p. 37, for Jane Spencer.
7 PCC (82 Hayes).
8 L. Hotson, *I, William Shakespeare* (1937), pp. 160, 244.
9 PRO, Req 2 111–16.
10 PCC (55 Dale).
11 *APC*, XIV, 97.
12 HMC, Hatfield House, VI, 19, 29, etc.
13 HMC, Hatfield House, XI, 404.

## IX. The Phoenix and the Turtle

1 Carleton Brown has shown, I think convincingly, that Sir John Salusbury, the

dedicatee, must be the turtle, and his wife the phoenix (*Poems of Sir John Salusbury and Robert Chester*, Early English Text Society, Extra Series, no. 113, 1914 (for 1913)). But there are other interpretations: A. B. Grosart, the editor of *Robert Chester's 'Loves Martyr'* (New Shakspere Society, 1878), argued that the phoenix and turtle represent Queen Elizabeth and the Earl of Essex, and William H. Matchett agreed (*The Phoenix and the Turtle*, 1965). Matchett, however, could not explain why Shakespeare should refer to Queen Elizabeth in the past tense in 1601; and Matchett seems not to have known J. E. Neale's studies of the Denbighshire elections (cf. p. 93), which contradict his theory that Salusbury could have been an Essex supporter. Roy T. Eriksen has suggested (*Spenser Studies*, 1981, II, 193–215) that Bruno's *De gli eroici furori* (1585) influenced Shakespeare's poem, which is possible; if he is right, 'the theory that Essex was the poem's turtle becomes highly improbable' (p. 210). But Eriksen's idea that the poem also alludes to 'the death of the Italian philosopher-poet at the stake in Rome' is surely far-fetched.

2  See *The Derby Household Books* (*The Stanley Papers*, Part II), ed. F. R. Raines (*CS*, 1853, vol. xxxi).

3  See 'Robert Parry's Diary' (*Archaeologia Cambrensis*, 1915, XV) p. 121. Matchett (*op. cit.*, p. 140) also prints a letter from the 6th Earl of Derby 'To my loving brother John Salusbury, Esq.', dated 1598.

4  Cf. Carleton Brown, p. lxxiii; Chambers, *Shakespeare*, I, 550.

5  See note 1.

6  Carleton Brown, p. 8.

7  HMC, Hatfield House, XI, 445 (24 Oct. 1601).

8  A. H. Dodd, 'North Wales in the Essex Revolt of 1601' (*EHR*, 1944, LIX, 368).

9  Lewys Dwnn, *Heraldic Visitations of Wales* (2 vols, Welsh Manuscripts Society, 1846), II, 331.

10  HMC, Hatfield House, IX, 180.

11  *Op. cit.*, IX, 181.

12  *DNB*; cf. J. Y. W. Lloyd, *The History of the Princes, The Lords Marcher, and the Ancient Nobility of Powys Fadog* (6 vols, 1881), IV, 307 ff.

13  PCC (41 Wallop).

14  Huntington Library, Ellesmere MSS., 669. According to Hasler (entry for Sir Robert Salesbury), Sir Robert asked Lord Keeper Egerton to be the guardian of his son.

15  Ellesmere MSS., 1782g.

16  Carleton Brown, p. lxix. Matchett disagrees with Brown's dating (p. 117, n.), but at this point ignores the piecemeal composition of *Love's Martyr*, about which he writes illuminatingly elsewhere.

17  For 'the Strong' see Lewys Dwnn (as in note 9). For Salusbury's formidable enemies see also the *Calendar of Salusbury Correspondence 1553 – circa 1700*, ed. W. J. Smith (Cardiff, 1954), pp. 30 ff.

18  Ellesmere MSS., no. 60.

19  Quoted by Carleton Brown, p. xxiv, n.

20  *SPD*, 270.48.

21  Carleton Brown, p. lxxi.

22  P. lxxiii.

23  P. lxix.

24  P. 125. My page references are to the 1601 edition of *Love's Martyr*.

25  Pp. 127–8.

26  P. lxiii.

27  For the rival theories about Shakespeare's commencement as a dramatist, 'early start' *v.* 'late start', see Honigmann, *Shakespeare's Impact on his Contemporaries*, pp. 53 ff.

28  First Folio, epistle.

29 There are good reasons for dating *Love's Labour's Lost* in 1592 or early 1593 (Honigmann, *op. cit.*, pp. 68–9).

30 Ed. 1635, p. 308.

31 *Op. cit.*, p. 112.

32 Cf. p. 119.

33 Camden, *Annals* (ed. 1635), p. 307.

34 Carleton Brown, p. 22; *DNB* (Thomas Stanley, first Earl of Derby).

35 Christ Church MS. 184, fo. 179b.

36 Carleton Brown, pp. 36, 37.

37 See the wills of Simon and Margaret Thelwall (PCC, 55 Windsor).

38 *The Autobiography of Edward Lord Herbert of Cherbury* (ed. S. Lee, 1888), p. 20.

39 P. xxv.

40 See also Penry Williams, *The Council in the Marches of Wales Under Elizabeth I* (Cardiff, 1958), pp. 124, 240, 285, etc.

41 *The Letters of John Chamberlain*, I, 61; *SPD*, James I, 2.2.

42 DDCl 915; papers deposited 24 Nov. 1954, DDCl 1108.

43 See the *Lleweni Estate Muniments* in the National Library of Wales, no. 516; Brown, p. xxv; also, the *Calendar of Salusbury Correspondence*, ed. W. J. Smith, pp. 9–10.

44 J. Y. W. Lloyd, *op. cit.*, VI, 432 ff. See PCC (126 Law) for Parry's will, and the *Lleweni Estate Muniments* (as in n. 43), nos. 807 and 808, for *Parry v. Salusbury*.

45 See *Archaeologia Cambrensis*, Sixth Series, 1905, V, 103–4.

46 J. P. Earwaker, ed., *Lancashire and Cheshire Wills and Inventories at Chester* (CS, New Series, 1884, III, 240).

47 See Chambers, *Shakespeare*, II, 234. The poem is in NLW MS. 5390. Mr G. C. G. Thomas of the National Library of Wales has kindly examined the MS. and writes (privately) that 'a number of hands belonging to the first half of the 17th century have contributed poems to the manuscript. Many of these were either composed by Sir Thomas Salusbury and Sir Henry Salusbury or addressed to them, and the majority of these are clearly holographs. The poem addressed to Heminges and Condell is anonymous in the manuscript but I believe it to be in the same hand as other poems in the manuscript to which the name "Henry Salusbury" or the initials "H.S." have been added.'

48 See *DNB*.

# X. Shakespeare's religion

1 Cf. p. 91

2 *Ancient Funeral Monuments*, p. 288.

3 Chambers, *Shakespeare*, II, 255–7.

4 Chambers, *Shakespeare*, I, 14.

5 See *Shakespeare Encyclopaedia*, p. 445.

6 Schoenbaum, *Documentary Life*, p. 37.

7 Cf. p. 2.

8 L. Hotson, *Shakespeare's Sonnets Dated*, p. 237.

9 Hotson, p. 227.

10 Hotson, *loc. cit.*

11 Chambers, *Shakespeare*, I, 15.

12 Chambers, *loc. cit.*

13 Schoenbaum, *op. cit.*, p. 41.

14 *Shakespeare Encyclopaedia*, p. 409.

15 *Shakespeare*, II, 380.

16 Cf. Schoenbaum, *Documentary Life*, pp. 41–7, and Chambers, *Shakespeare*, II, 381.

# Notes

17 *Shakespeare Encyclopaedia*, p. 753.
18 E. I. Fripp argued that John Shakespeare withdrew from the Stratford 'halls' in 1577 because of The Grand Commission Ecclesiastical (1575) and its hunting out of recusants; Fripp, however, thought that John Shakespeare was a Puritan (*Minutes and Accounts of the Corporation of Stratford-upon-Avon and other Records 1553–1620*, 3 vols, Dugdale Society, 1921–6; II, xlv ff.). See also J. H. de Groot's careful survey of the evidence in *The Shakespeares and 'The Old Faith'* (New York, 1946).
19 Chambers, *Shakespeare*, II, 20.
20 Leatherbarrow, *Elizabethan Recusants*, p. 43.
21 Coward, *The Stanleys*, p. 167.
22 *APC*, XV, 361.
23 See *King John*, New Arden ed., pp. 155, 63–4; and G. Bullough, *Narrative and Dramatic Sources of Shakespeare* (8 vols, 1957 etc.), IV, 98.
24 Honigmann, *Shakespeare's Impact*, pp. 53–90.
25 See Kenneth Muir's New Arden edition of *King Lear*.
26 Chambers, *Shakespeare*, II, 175.
27 Chambers, II, 256.

# XI. Conclusion

1 Cf. Baldwin, *Small Latine*, I, 464 ff. Simon Hunt, the Stratford schoolmaster from 1571 to 1575, later became a Jesuit; Thomas Jenkins (1575–9) had been a Fellow of Campion's college (St John's, Oxford), a college that had treated Catholics with tolerance (Baldwin, I, 486); John Cottom (1579–81) was brother of the Jesuit Thomas Cottam.
2 *Shakespeare's Impact* (1982).
3 Honigmann, *op. cit.*, pp. 1–14.
4 *APC*, XVII, 95.
5 Chambers, *Shakespeare*, II, 266–7.
6 Shakespeare's First Folio, dedication.
7 Miller, *Hoghton Tower*, p. 222.

# Appendix C. *A Midsummer Night's Dream*, *Henry VI* Parts 2 and 3, and the Stanley family

1 See Chambers, *Shakespeare*, I, 359, and 'The Occasion of *A Midsummer Night's Dream*' (in *Gleanings*).
2 See Honigmann, *Shakespeare's Impact on his Contemporaries* (1982), p. 77.
3 Chambers, *Gleanings*, p. 63.
4 See Coward, *The Stanleys*, and Lefranc, *Sous le Masque*.
5 *SPD*, 271.35.
6 This is the accepted date, confirmed by Mr J. J. Bagley, the author of a forthcoming book about the Earls of Derby.
7 H. H. Goldstine, *New and Full Moons 1001 B.C. to A.D. 1651* (Memoirs of the American Philosophical Society, vol. 94. Philadelphia, 1973).
8 Chambers, *Gleanings*, p. 61.
9 B. M. Ward, *The Seventeenth Earl of Oxford 1550–1604* (1928), pp. 317 ff.
10 Huntington Library, Ellesmere MSS., no. 213.
11 F. A. Bailey, 'Some Stanley Heraldic Glass from Worden Hall, Lancashire' (*HSLC*, 1950 (for 1949), CI, 69).
12 Harold Brooks, ed. *A Midsummer Night's Dream* (New Arden, 1979), pp. xxxiv–xxxv.

13 G. Bullough, *Narrative and Dramatic Sources of Shakespeare*, vol. 3 (1960), p. 161.
14 K. Muir, *The Sources of Shakespeare's Plays* (1977), p. 27.

# Index

Abbot, John, 141
Adams, Mrs Richard, 29
Adderley, William, 143
Admiral's Men, 59, 63, 159
'Aetion', 75
Ainsworth, Harrison, 14
Alexander, Peter, 60–1, 120, 159
Allen, Cardinal, 11, 24
Alleyn, Edward, 18
Alty, Lawrence, 34
'Amaryllis', 75
Ambrose, William, 41–2, 48
Amias, John, 140
'Amyntas', 75
Anderson, Roger, 155
Anderton, Roger, 10
Anstruther, Godfrey, 139
Armin, Robert, 18
Arundel, Earl of, 119
Arundel, Sir John, 119
Ascroft, William, 137
Ashcroft, Philip, 34
Ashton, Dorothy, 28, 140
Ashton, Richard, 28
Aspeden, John, 141
Aspinall, Alexander, 40, 131–2
Aubrey, John, 2–3, 126, 155
Audeley, John, 115
Awly, Thomas, 86, 143

Babington, A., 91, 102, 106, 122
Backhouse, Thomas, 142
Bagley, J. J., 32, 163
Bailey, F. A., 152, 163
Baker, Oliver, 28–9, 135
Baker, Richard, 142, 155
Baldwin, T. W., 5–6, 40 ff., 155, 157, 163
Bamvile, P. de, 152
Bannister, George, 137
Bannister, Henry, 51, 157
Bannister, Richard, 138–9, 140
Barker, Thomas, 137
Barlow, Margaret, 119
Barnfield, Richard, 54, 74
Barton, Thomas, 17, 23, 137–9, 140
Bastard, Thomas, 55

Beamont, W., 156
Beaufort, Cardinal, 119
Beeston, Christopher, 3, 59
Beeston, William, 2–3, 21, 127
Bennett, J. H. E., 32
Benson, John, 141
Berain, Catherine of, 91–2, 108–9, 149
Berkeley, Thomas, 150
Beseley, Ellen, 139
Beseley, George, 9, 135 ff., 139
Beseley, John, 137
Bess of Hardwick, 80, 160
Betterton, Thomas, 2
Blacklatch, Adam, 141
Blundell, Richard, 20
Blundell, William, 20
Bolton, Robert, 137
Bolton, Thomas, 141
Bond, Henry, 17, 137, 139
Borromeo, Carlo, 117
Boulton, Adam, 138
Brasenose College, 40
Bretton, 17, 46
Brewer, Ann, 41
Bronte, Charlotte, 156
Bronte, Patrick, 20
Brooke-Little, J. P., 132
Brooks, Harold, 150, 153, 163
Brown, Carleton, 91 ff., 160 ff.
Brown, George, 44, 46, 145
Brown, Jane, 44–5
Browne, Anne, 10
Browne, Henry, 137
Browne, Roger, 10
Bruno, G., 161
Bryan, George, 59
'Brynscowes', 12, 136
Bullough, G., 154, 163–4
Burbage, Richard, 59, 83
Burbage, William, 115
Burgh, Nicholas, 81
Burghley, Lord, 20, 24, 95, 119
Butler pedigree, 147
Butler, Ann, 51, 158
Butler, Henry, 7, 51, 53, 58, 114, 157–8
Butler, Nicholas, 52
Butler, Nicholas ii, 157

[165]

# Index

# Index

# Index

# Index

# Index

# Index